SCHOLASTIC

AMAZING
ANIMAL
ART PROJECTS

20 Easy Step-by-Step Paper Projects
That Connect to Seasonal and Science Topics

by Jo Lynn Alcorn

New York • Toronto • London • Auckland • Sydney
Mexico City • New Delhi • Hong Kong • Buenos Aires

Teaching *Resources*

This book is dedicated to my dog, Copper—
beloved family member
and truly amazing animal.

Edited and produced by Immacula A. Rhodes
Cover design by Jo Lynn Alcorn
Interior design and illustrations by Jo Lynn Alcorn
Writing activities and book lists by Alyse Sweeney

ISBN-13: 978-0-439-51786-7
ISBN-10: 0-439-51786-9

Copyright © 2008 by Jo Lynn Alcorn
Published by Scholastic Inc.
All rights reserved.
Printed in China.

1 2 3 4 5 6 7 8 9 10   62   15 14 13 12 11 10 09 08

Contents

Fall

Winter

Spring

Summer

Introduction

From birth, children seem to have a natural interest in the animal world. Animals provide them with a source of inspiration and stimulation—from the visual to the tactile—as they learn and grow.

From the elegance of a dragonfly in flight to the comic waddling of the penguin, animals are beauty in motion. From the brilliant markings of a tropical fish to the subtlety of the white snowshoe hare against the snow, they are a visual delight. From the hibernation of the bear to the migration of the monarch butterfly, they are a lesson in the practicalities of survival. And from the fierceness of an alligator to the timid meekness of a mouse, they span a range of behaviors that often seem to parallel that of humans.

The projects in this book are designed to connect art to the animals that are typically introduced in your science or seasonal studies. You can use the projects to enrich your lessons about animals and their characteristics, behaviors, and habitats. In addition, all the activities help support you in meeting the standards outlined by Mid-continent Research for Education and Learning (McREL) for art and science (see page 7).

The art techniques used in creating the 3-D animals are quite basic, and the materials are easy to prepare. Before starting each project, you might want to ask children to share what they know about the selected animal to stimulate a thoughtful discussion about the creature and its characteristics. Then, as they make the animal, encourage children to talk about its special features, as well as the materials and process they use to construct it.

Please feel free to use these projects as taking-off points for your class. Encourage invention, individuality, and innovation. Don't be afraid to experiment— and above all, have fun!

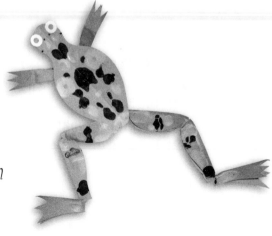

—*Jo Lynn Alcorn*

How to Use This Book

Amazing Animal Art Projects includes projects that can be used during every season of the year, reproducible patterns needed to make the projects, and literacy activities that reinforce writing skills.

The Projects

The projects in this book are organized by the four seasons. The pages for each project provide all you need to know to make the animal—from preparation to finished product. Here's an overview of what you will find in each unit:

Materials

A complete, easy-to-read list of the materials each child needs to make the project is provided in this section. Most of the items are readily available, inexpensive, and easy to prepare and use.

What to Do

The step-by-step instructions given in this section tell you how to construct the project. Easy-to-read diagrams and illustrations help make the process go smoothly.

Tip

These useful tips include variations, shortcuts, and safety measures to consider when making the project.

Write About It!

A project-related writing activity is provided to help reinforce or expand children's writing skills.

Nonfiction Literature Links

You can use the books in this section with the writing activity, to introduce the animal before making the project, to reinforce what children already know about the animal, or to add to their knowledge base.

Reproducible Pages

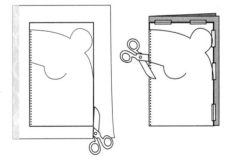

Easy-to-cut-out pattern boxes are included for many of the projects. To use these, children cut out the box before beginning construction of their project. They tape the pattern box to another sheet of paper as specified in the directions and then cut out the shape inside the box. Bold, dotted lines are provided on some pattern boxes to indicate where the pattern should be placed on a fold. With this system, children cut out the shape only once. In most cases, the excess paper from the pattern box will fall away as the shape is being cut out. Children can carefully remove any pattern or tape that remains attached to the shape after it has been cut out.

Some projects call for color-and-cut patterns. These patterns are provided for "Migrating Monarch," "Masked Raccoon," "Observant Owl," "Fish Mobile," and "Colorful Beetle." To use this kind of pattern, children simply color it and then cut it out for direct use in the project.

How to Display

From bulletin board ideas to dioramas, you can use the unique and inviting ideas presented in this section to showcase children's creations in the classroom.

Tips for Managing the Projects

Take time to construct each project yourself before presenting it to children. This will help you to become familiar with the materials, steps, and time it takes to complete the project. And you can use the finished project as a model to inspire and motivate children. When planning, you might also consider the time needed for preparation, setup, and cleanup.

Prepare enough materials for each child to have all the items needed to complete the project. You'll want to include extra materials, as well, to have on hand for mistakes and so that you can make the project along with children to demonstrate each step. As you guide children through the process, take one step at a time, and wait for them to complete each step before proceeding to the next one. If desired, save the larger pieces of paper for future use in collages and other projects.

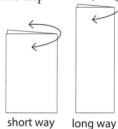

A Word About Folding

Many of the projects give directions for folding paper. When you read "fold the paper the short way," the paper will be folded widthwise (like a hamburger bun). For "fold the paper the long way," fold the paper lengthwise (like a hotdog bun).

short way   long way

Discussion Starters

Here are some prompts you can use to initiate a discussion about the animals featured in this book.

Physical Traits

- Describe the animal's appearance.
- What kind of outer covering does it have? (for example, fur, feathers, scales)
- Tell about any special characteristics that help the animal survive. (spots, a shell, large eyes)

Classification

- What group does the animal belong to? (mammal, bird, insect)
- Why does it belong to this group?
- How is the animal similar to or different from other animals in the same group?

Lifestyle and Habits

- What does the animal eat? (plants, insects, other animals)
- How does it get its food? (gather, forage, hunt)
- What special features help it obtain food? (night vision, sharp claws, quiet movement)
- How does it avoid danger? (camouflage, deceptive patterning, swift flyer)

Behavior

- How does the animal get around? (walks, swims, flies)
- What sound, if any, does the animal make?
- Does it hibernate, migrate, or stay active in the winter?

Growth and Development

- Does the animal lay eggs? Or does it give birth to live young?
- How does the young animal change as it grows into an adult?
- Tell about the animal's life cycle.

Environment

- Where does the animal live? (forest, swamp, polar region)
- What are some special features of its habitat?
- Name some characteristics that help the animal survive in its environment. (thick fur, echolocation, webbed feet for swimming)

Connections to the Standards

This book is designed to support you in meeting the following art and science standards outlined by Mid-continent Research for Education and Learning (McREL), an organization that collects and synthesizes national and state standards.

Art

Understands and applies media, techniques, and processes related to the visual arts

- Knows the differences between art materials, techniques, and processes
- Knows how different media, techniques, and processes are used to communicate ideas, experiences, and stories
- Knows how different materials, techniques, and processes cause different responses from the viewer
- Uses art materials and tools in a safe and responsible manner

Knows how to use structures (e.g., sensory qualities, organizational principles, expressive features) and functions of art

- Knows the differences among visual characteristics and purposes of art
- Uses visual structures and functions of art to communicate ideas

Knows a range of subject matter, symbols, and potential ideas in the visual arts

- Selects prospective ideas (e.g., formulated thoughts, opinions, concepts) for works of art
- Knows how subject matter, symbols, and ideas are used to communicate meaning

Understands the characteristics and merits of one's own artwork and the artwork of others

- Knows various purposes for creating works of visual art
- Understands that specific artworks can elicit different responses

Science

Understands the principles of heredity and related concepts

- Knows that differences exist among individuals of the same kind of animal

Understands the structure and function of cells and organisms

- Knows that animals have features that help them live in different environments
- Knows that living organisms have distinct structures and body systems that serve specific functions in growth and survival
- Knows that the behavior of individual organisms is influenced by internal cues (e.g., hunger) and external cues (e.g., changes in the environment)

Understands relationships among organisms and their physical environment

- Knows that animals need certain resources for energy and growth
- Knows that living things are found almost everywhere in the world and that distinct environments support the life of different types of animals
- Knows that an organism's patterns of behavior are related to the nature of that organism's environment

Understands biological evolution and the diversity of life

- Knows that there are similarities and differences in the appearance and behavior of animals
- Knows different ways in which living things can be grouped and purposes of different groupings

Source: Kendall, J. S., & Marzano, R. J. (2004). *Content knowledge: A compendium of standards and benchmarks for K–12 education.* Aurora, CO: Mid-continent Research for Education and Learning. Online database: http://www.mcrel.org/standards-benchmarks

Migrating Monarch

Every fall, millions of monarch butterflies migrate to the warmer climates of Mexico and California. After children make their own butterflies in bright and vivid colors, they can group them together on boughs to form a butterfly cluster.

Materials

For each child:

* butterfly pattern (page 58)
* 9- by 12 -inch green construction paper (for leaf)
* 1 ½- by 15-inch length of green posterboard (for every 5 leaves)

Other materials:

* scissors
* bright yellow and orange crayons or markers
* glue stick
* black marker
* stapler

Tip

To make one long bough, add six inches to the posterboard strip for every two leaves you want to add to it.

What to Do

Make a copy of the pattern for each child. Pass out the materials. Have children cut out the pattern box. Then demonstrate the following steps.

Butterfly

1 Color the front and back of the butterfly. Fold the pattern along the dotted line and glue the sides together. When the glue dries, cut out the butterfly. If needed, touch up the edges with the black marker.

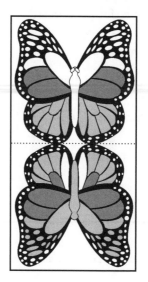

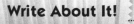

2 Fold the front wings toward each other to make the butterfly appear to flutter.

Bough

3 To make a leaf, fold the 9- by 12-inch paper in half the long way. Cut out a large half-oval, starting and ending at the fold.

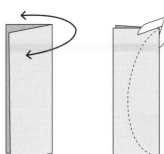

4 Collect each child's leaf. To make a bough, staple five leaves to a 15-inch-long posterboard strip. Make as many boughs as needed to use all the leaves. Or see "Tip" (page 8) to make one long bough.

5 Collect each child's butterfly. Use one staple per butterfly to attach each child's monarch to a bough. If you want to display a butterfly in a closed-wing position, fold it in half and staple it to the leaf along its body.

Flutter and fly, butterfly!

Staple the boughs to a bulletin board or tape them on or around a door.

Share with children information about the monarch's incredible migrating journey. Then read aloud *Butterflies Fly* (see below). Point out how each five-line poem ends in a sentence following this pattern: "That's _____ butterflies fly," using *how*, *when*, *where*, or *why* to fill in the blank. Have children use the book as a model to write their own five-line poems about the migrating monarch.

Nonfiction Literature Links

Butterflies Fly by Yvonne Winer (Charlesbridge Publishing, 2000). This unique book features a five-line poem on each spread and beautifully explores how, when, where, and why butterflies fly.

The Journey of a Butterfly by Carolyn Scrace (Franklin Watts, 2000). Bright illustrations and a map help break down the monarch's migration into the different stages of the journey.

Courageous Crow

Crows are large, strong, inquisitive, and adaptable birds. They are as much at home in urban settings as on farms. Flocks of crows, often comical in their noisy behavior, are a common sight in early fall. But farmers don't think crows are funny—they use scarecrows to keep the pesky birds away from crops. Although this realistic crow can flap its wings, it is quite unflappable!

Materials

For each child:

- crow patterns (page 59)
- 12- by 18-inch black construction paper
- 9-inch square of black construction paper
- 2 hole reinforcements
- 5-inch square of yellow or orange construction paper
- two 9- by 12-inch sheets of black construction paper

Other materials:

- scissors
- clear tape
- stapler
- glue stick

Tip

If desired, work with small groups to help children make their crows. Or challenge several children to work together to make one crow.

What to Do

Make a copy of the patterns for each child. Pass out the materials. Have children cut out the pattern boxes. Then demonstrate the following steps.

Body and Tail

1 Fold the 12- by 18-inch paper in half the long way. Tape the head pattern to the paper, as shown. Cut out the gray shape and discard it. Carefully remove the pattern and tape.

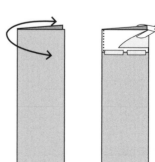

2 Open the paper and fold in the corners, as shown. Unfold the two bottom corners and fold each one in half again. Tape the bottom corners in place.

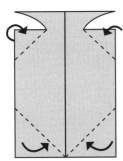 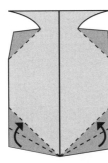 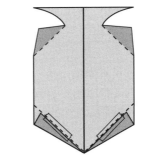

3 Accordion-fold the 9-inch square of black paper. Staple one end of the folded paper. Tape the tail to the body, as shown.

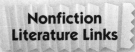

4 Overlap and staple the bottom corners together. Repeat with the top corners.

5 Cut away the point at the top of the head, rounding the head as you cut. Add hole reinforcements for eyes.

Beak

6 Fold the 5-inch square of yellow or orange paper in half. Tape the beak pattern along the fold, as shown. Cut out the triangle.

7 Apply glue to the inside of the folded triangle and fit it over the crow's beak.

Wings

8 Stack together the two sheets of 9- by 12-inch black paper. Cut out large wings through both layers, as shown. Then cut fringes along the curved sides, leaving about 4 inches at the top of the wings.

9 Place a wing on each side of the body, as shown. Staple them in place close to the ridge of the crow's back.

Tip

To keep the wings in a raised position, paper-clip them together above the crow's body.

10 To make the wings flap, hold the crow near the base of its tail and move it up and down rapidly.

Fly, crow, fly!

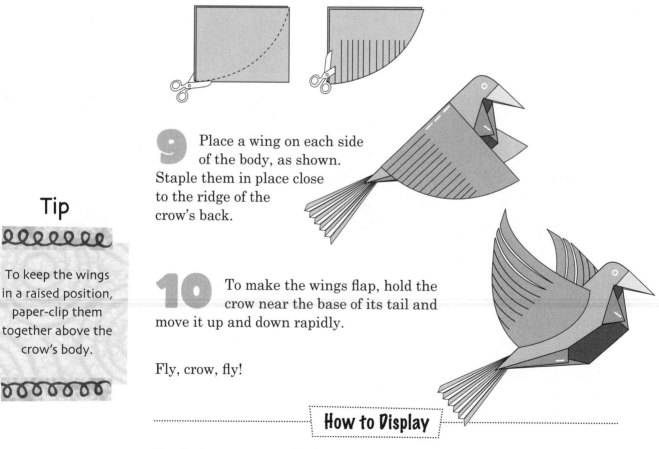

How to Display

Perch the crows on a bookshelf, windowsill, or even the back of a chair. Or use string to suspend them from the ceiling.

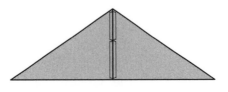

Bat Hat

Bats are nocturnal and use echolocation to sense the walls of their dark caves. These winged mammals pollinate trees and plants as they fly around. They also help control the insect population. Children can wear these unique bat hats to share their bat knowledge with others.

Materials

For each child:

- two 12- by-18 inch sheets of black construction paper
- 2 hole reinforcements

Other materials:

- white or light crayon
- 24-inch ruler or straight edge
- clear tape
- scissors
- stapler

Tip

If desired, cut out feet from black paper. Then tape the feet to the bottom of the completed bat.

What to Do

Pass out the materials. Then demonstrate the following steps.

Head and Body

1 Stack the black papers. Using the ruler and crayon, draw a diagonal line from corner to corner on the top sheet.

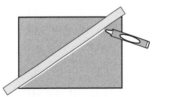

2 Cut along the line through both sheets. When finished, you will have two sets of triangles.

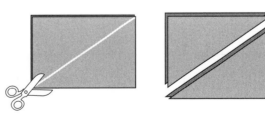

3 Flip over one of the triangles in a set. Position and tape the two shapes together to make one large triangle, as shown.

Write About It!

After sharing Gail Gibbons' *Bats* (see below), invite children to work together to create a class alphabet book about bats. Challenge them to come up with a bat fact for each letter of the alphabet, such as *echolocation* for *e*. (Gibbons' book contains terms such as *nocturnal*, *membrane*, and *roosts*— all great words for a bat alphabet book!) Then have children write a brief explanation of each fact. You might provide a variety of alphabet books for children to use as inspiration.

Nonfiction Literature Links

Bats
by Gail Gibbons
(Holiday House, 2000).
Gibbons explores all aspects of a bat's life, including echolocation, hibernation, and natural habitats.

Bats
by Lily Wood
(Scholastic, 2001).
Gorgeous photographs enhance the author's introduction to the fascinating world of bats.

4 To make the head, fold down the top 3 inches of the triangle. Starting at each side, cut along the fold about halfway to the center.

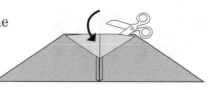

5 Fold up the loose corners of the cut section to create ears. Add hole reinforcements for eyes.

Wings

6 Repeat step 3 with the other set of triangles. Position the large triangle as shown.

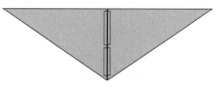

7 To make realistic-looking wings, fold the triangle in half. Cut scallops along the long edge, as shown, cutting through both layers.

8 Unfold the wings. Center the body on top of the wings. Then staple the body in place at the "shoulders."

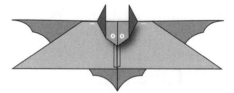

9 To make the hat, help each child overlap the bottom corners of the body so that the bat fits around his or her head. Tape the ends in place.

Put your bat hat on and dart away!

.... **How to Display** ....

Wrap the wings around the bat body and fasten them together with a paper clip. Then convert your classroom into a bat cave by suspending the bats upside down from the ceiling.

Masked Raccoon

Raccoons, seen in city and country alike, are known for their mischievous ways. These nocturnal masked marauders use their human-like hands to gather and clean their food. When children make this cute raccoon critter, will they be able to keep it out of trouble?

Materials

For each child:

- raccoon patterns (page 60)
- 8- by 14-inch white posterboard
- 1- by 6-inch white posterboard
- 2- by 12-inch black construction paper
- three 2- by 3-inch pieces of white construction paper
- three 2- by 3-inch pieces of black construction paper

Other materials:

- brown, gray, and black crayons or markers
- scissors
- clear tape
- glue stick

Tip

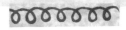

To make a quick-and-easy tail, color black stripes on a 2- by 12-inch strip of white construction paper. Round off one end and then attach the other end to the raccoon.

What to Do

Make a copy of the patterns for each child. Pass out the materials. Then demonstrate the following steps.

Head

1 Color the head brown or gray and add whiskers. Cut out the head.

2 Fold the head in half and then unfold it. Fold the ears forward toward the face.

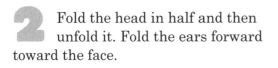

Body and Paws

3 Fold the 8- by 14-inch posterboard in half the short way. To make the body, round off the corners of one of the panels, as shown. Color in brown or gray "fur" on that panel.

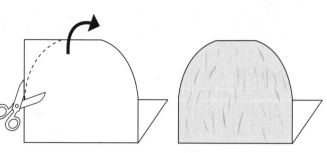

4 Stand the body upright and turn the colored side away from you. Fold the base panel in half toward the body.

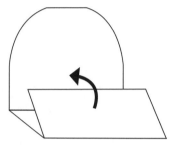

5 To make the stand, tape the end of the base to the back of the body, as shown. The base will form a triangle and the body will tilt back at an angle.

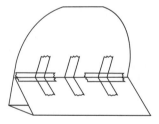

6 Tape one end of the 1- by 6-inch posterboard strip to the back of the body to create a neck, as shown. Then fold down the top 1 $\frac{1}{2}$ inches of the loose end to form a tab. Apply glue to the tab and attach the head.

7 Cut out the paws. Carefully cut along the dashed lines to form the fingers. Then fold the paws where indicated. Glue each paw to the body, as shown.

Tail

8 Round off one end of the 2- by 12-inch black paper strip. Cut a 2-inch fringe on the rounded end, as shown.

9 Stack and fringe the 2- by 3-inch white papers, cutting through all layers. Repeat with the 2- by 3-inch black papers. Glue the fringed papers onto the tail, alternating the two colors, as shown. Then tape the tail to the inside of the base of the raccoon.

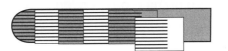

Now your raccoon is ready to scavenge the neighborhood!

How to Display

Invite children to make a name card to tape between their raccoon's hands. Or have them attach a small lightweight object for their critter to hold on to.

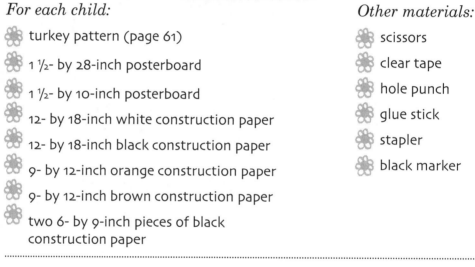

Turkey Topper

Wild turkeys, the largest birds of the forest, forage for insects and berries during the day. Then they fly up to low branches to sleep at night. Children will enjoy wearing this turkey hat as they share their turkey knowledge with others.

Tip

To simplify the tail fan, use only the 12- by 18-inch white construction paper in step 2. Then use black, white, and orange markers to color 1-inch-wide bands along the curved edge of the tail fan.

Materials

For each child:

❀ turkey pattern (page 61)

❀ 1 ½- by 28-inch posterboard

❀ 1 ½- by 10-inch posterboard

❀ 12- by 18-inch white construction paper

❀ 12- by 18-inch black construction paper

❀ 9- by 12-inch orange construction paper

❀ 9- by 12-inch brown construction paper

❀ two 6- by 9-inch pieces of black construction paper

Other materials:

❀ scissors

❀ clear tape

❀ hole punch

❀ glue stick

❀ stapler

❀ black marker

What to Do

Make a copy of the pattern for each child. Pass out the materials. Have children cut out the pattern box. Then demonstrate the following steps.

Headband

1 Help each child overlap the ends of the 28-inch strip of posterboard until it fits around his or her head. Tape the ends in place. Then securely tape the 10-inch posterboard strip to the headband so that it stands upright like a post.

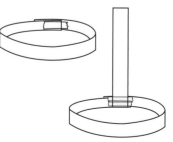

Tail

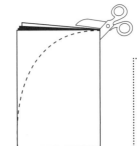

2 To make tail fans, stack the 12- by 18-inch black and white papers and then fold them in half the short way. Round off one corner opposite the fold, as shown, cutting through all layers of paper. Separate the tail fans.

3 Unfold and tape the black tail fan to the post on the headband, as shown.

4 With the white tail fan folded, cut away about 1 ½ inches from the curved edged, cutting through both layers.

5 Repeat step 2 using the single piece of orange paper. Then nest and glue the white and orange tail fans together. Fold the tail fan unit in half and cut a 2-inch long slit about an inch away from the fold, as shown.

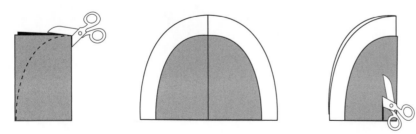

6 Unfold the white and orange tail fan. Place it in front of the black tail fan, fitting the slits over the rim of the headband and taping it in place, as shown.

Write About It!

Read aloud *The First Thanksgiving* (see below) and discuss the foods that were most likely enjoyed by the participants at the Harvest Feast. Then invite children to wear their turkey toppers and pretend to be turkeys. Have them write a letter, from the turkey's perspective, to persuade Americans to eat foods other than turkey on Thanksgiving Day. They might suggest serving foods such as deer, goose, clams, fish, and lobster, or even including more vegetable dishes in the feast.

Nonfiction Literature Links

All About Turkeys by Jim Arnosky (Scholastic, 1998). Illustrations and informative text provide a wealth of information about wild turkeys.

The First Thanksgiving by Linda Hayward (Random House, 1990). This illustrated book tells the story of the Harvest Feast and includes a menu of foods possibly served during the celebration.

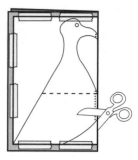

Body

7 Fold the brown paper in half the short way. Tape the body pattern to the paper, as shown. Cut out the body through both layers. Punch a hole for the eyes where indicated. Fold and then unfold the body along the dotted line. Remove the pattern.

Tip

For a tom turkey, cut a snood and wattle from red paper. Glue the snood to the top base of the beak and the wattle between the two sides of the neck just under the beak.

8 Staple together the two sides of the head at the top and the chest above the fold, as shown. Draw a beak with the black marker. Then open up the body so that the turkey's chest pushes outward.

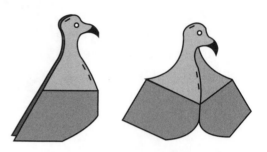

9 Tape the body to the headband, as shown.

Wings

10 Stack the two 6- by 9-inch black papers. Cutting through both layers, round off one corner, as shown. Cut a 4-inch fringe along the short straight edge. Separate the wings and glue them to the body.

Time to put on your turkey topper and strut your stuff!

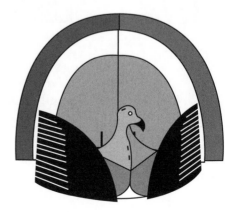

Snooze-and-Wake Bear

Winter is here and it's time for bears to hibernate! With this unique pop-out card, children can wake the bear by opening its eyes and then close them again when it's time for a long winter snooze!

Materials

For each child:
- bear patterns (pages 62–63)
- 9- by 12-inch colored construction paper (for card)
- 9- by 12-inch brown construction paper
- two 2 ½-inch squares of black construction paper
- 2 hole reinforcements
- 8-inch square of brown construction paper

Other materials:
- scissors
- crayons or markers
- clear tape
- glue stick

Tip

Although polar bears don't hibernate, you might invite children to make a white bear as part of a unit on Arctic animals.

What to Do

Make a copy of the patterns for each child. Pass out the materials. Have children cut out the pattern boxes. Then demonstrate the following steps.

Card

1 Fold the colored paper in half the short way. Draw a forest scene on the front of the card. Then set the card aside for use in step 5.

Head

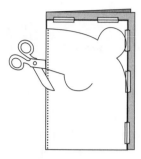

2 Fold the 9- by 12-inch brown paper in half the short way. Tape the head pattern to the paper along the fold, as shown. Cut along the solid line for the bear's eyelids. Then cut out the head.

3 Unfold the head with the fold pointing down to form a valley. Fold the eyelids back to create openings for the eyes, as shown. Draw eyelashes around the eye openings. Then color the inside of the ears. Fold each ear forward toward the face.

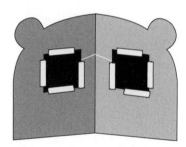

4 Turn the head facedown and tape a black square over each eye opening.

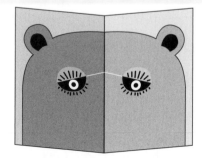

5 Turn the head faceup and add hole reinforcements to create eyes. Then open the card, fit the head into the fold, and glue it in place, making sure the card closes and opens easily. Do not glue the eyelids or ears.

Muzzle

6 Fold the 8-inch brown square in half. Tape the muzzle pattern along the fold, as shown. Cut out the muzzle. Then unfold it so that the fold points up to form a peak. Draw a nose and mouth on the muzzle.

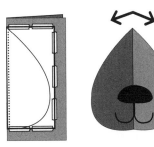

7 Turn the muzzle facedown. Stick a piece of tape—sticky side down—on each side of the muzzle, allowing the tape to extend over the edge, as shown.

8 Fold the muzzle with the plain side on the inside. Line up the fold of the muzzle with the straight line across the top of the eye, as shown. Then close the card and press firmly so that the tape on the muzzle sticks to the inside of the card.

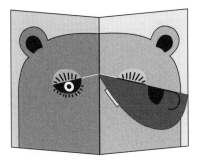

When you open the card, the bear's muzzle will pop out! You can open and close its eyelids to make the bear wake or sleep.

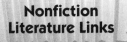

Playful Penguin

Penguins are aquatic birds that can't fly. Their wings are used like flippers as they swim around the sea. When walking across land, penguins use their feet and big tail to maintain their balance. This three-dimensional penguin captures the fun and playfulness of this beloved bird, from its white belly to its "topcoat and tails" and amusing waddle!

Tip

eeeeeee

If desired, work with small groups to help children make their penguins. Or challenge several children to work together to make one penguin.

oooooooo

Materials

For each child:

- penguin pattern (page 64)
- 12- by 18-inch white construction paper
- two 12- by 18-inch sheets of black construction paper
- 2 hole reinforcements
- 6- by 9-inch yellow construction paper

Other materials:

- scissors
- stapler
- white crayon
- clear tape

What to Do

Make a copy of the pattern for each student. Pass out the materials. Have children cut out the pattern box. Then demonstrate the following steps.

Body and Tail

1 To make the belly, overlap the short ends of the white paper about two inches to form a tube, as shown. Staple the ends in place at the top and bottom of the tube. Then pinch one end of the tube closed and staple once in the middle. Stand the tube upright with the seam away from you.

2 For the "topcoat," fold a 12- by 18-inch sheet of black paper in half the long way. Line up the top of the belly tube with the top edge of the paper, as shown. Use the white crayon to mark the length of the tube on the black paper.

3 Unfold the paper and cut along the fold to the crayon mark. Fold in and tape the bottom corners in place, as shown, to form pointed flaps. Then fold each flap back to form the tail.

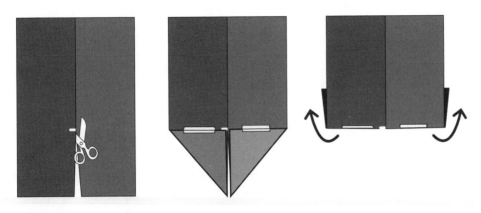

4 Center the topcoat behind the belly, as shown. Staple the pieces together at the top using only one staple in the middle. Wrap the top corners of the topcoat around to the front of the belly and staple in place.

Wings and Head

5 Fold the remaining 12- by 18-inch sheet of black paper in half the short way. Tape the head pattern to the paper along the fold, as shown. Cut along the diagonal line, cutting through all layers. Then carefully remove the pattern and tape.

6 Unfold the paper. To make wings, fold down the top flap on each side of the center fold, as shown. Place the wings over the body, fitting the top corners of the body under the wing flaps. Staple the wings in place at the "shoulders."

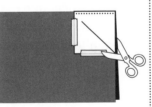

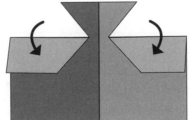

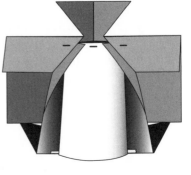

7 Fold down the top corner of each wing and staple. Then fold each wing forward again, as shown.

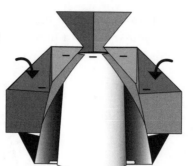
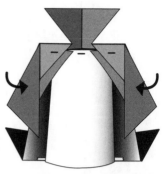

8 For the head, pull together the two corners of the paper that extends above the body. Staple the edges together along the top edge. To make eyes, add a hole reinforcement to each side of the head. Trim away the top point to round off the head.

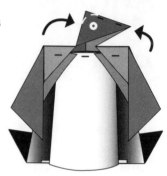

Beak and Feet

9 Cut off a corner of the 6- by 9- inch yellow paper for the beak. Fold the beak in half, as shown. Then slip it over the penguin's nose, glue it in place, and trim it to fit.

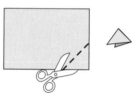

10 To make the feet, cut two 2-inch-wide rectangles from the yellow paper. Stack the rectangles and cut a long, narrow wedge from each side (as shown), cutting through both layers of paper. Fold up about 1 inch of the narrow end of each foot. Glue the folded end of each foot to the inside of the bottom of the body.

Stand the penguin on the table and tilt it from side to side as you move it forward. Time to waddle away, penguin!

Snowshoe Hare

It's a favorite but rare sight—the white on white of the snowshoe hare against the snow. This white hopper uses its strong back feet to leap into action to escape its predators. But children can make this adorable hare that won't dash away!

Materials

For each child:

❁ hare patterns (pages 65–66)

❁ 9- by 12-inch white construction paper

❁ 6- by 9-inch white construction paper

❁ 2 hole reinforcements

Other materials:

❁ scissors

❁ clear tape

❁ markers or crayons

❁ glue stick

❁ stapler

Tip

To make a summer weather snowshoe hare, have children use brown construction paper instead of white.

What to Do

Make a copy of the patterns for each child. Pass out the materials. Have children cut out the pattern boxes. Then demonstrate the following steps.

Body

1 Fold the 9- by 12-inch paper in half the short way. Tape the body pattern to the paper along the fold, as shown. Cut out the body.

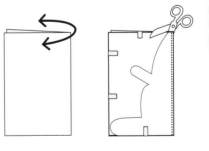

2 Unfold the body with the fold facing downward to form a valley. Fold the small paws toward each other. Draw toe lines on the small and large paws.

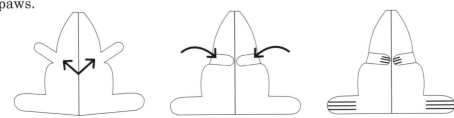

3 Fold the large paws up toward the body. Then unfold them and cut a slit along the vertical fold line up to the horizontal fold line, as shown.

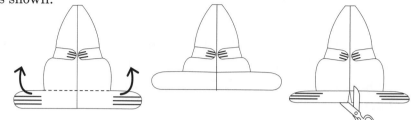

4 Pull the heels of the large paws together until they overlap. Tape them in place and then stand the body up on the large paws.

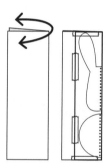

Head and Tail

5 Fold the 6- by 9-inch paper in half the long way. Tape the head and tail patterns to the paper along the fold, as shown. Cut out the shapes.

6 Unfold the tail and glue it to the base of the body.

7 Unfold the head so that the fold points up to form a peak. Add hole reinforcements for eyes and color in the pupils. Draw a nose and whiskers on the head. To contour the ears, fold each one down the middle toward the front.

8 Staple the head to the body, as shown.

Now, this big foot is ready to hop away!

Observant Owl

With its large eyes, an owl has excellent night vision and can turn its head to look from side to side and behind its back. Children can rotate the head of this Great Horned Owl hand puppet to help it search for food, as well as a place for winter nesting.

Materials

For each child:

- owl eyes (page 66)
- 7- by 12-inch white construction paper
- 9-inch square of black construction paper
- 6- by 15-inch white construction paper
- 6-inch square of brown construction paper
- 8-inch length of yarn

Other materials:

- stapler
- scissors
- crayons or markers
- glue stick
- clear tape

What to Do

Make a copy of the owl eyes for each student. Pass out all the materials. Then demonstrate the following steps.

Body

1 To make the body, overlap the short ends of the 7- by 12-inch white paper to form a tube that fits over your forearm and is large enough to slide your hand through. Staple the ends in place.

2 For feathers, fold the black square in half. Cutting through both layers, round off one corner opposite the fold. Unfold and fringe the curved end, as shown.

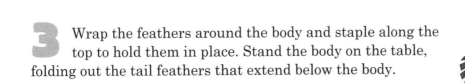

3 Wrap the feathers around the body and staple along the top to hold them in place. Stand the body on the table, folding out the tail feathers that extend below the body.

Tip

To protect children's hands, cover the staples on the inside of the owl's body with tape.

Write About It!

Discuss with children the attributes that make owls such incredible birds of prey—their excellent vision, keen hearing, hooked beaks, sharp claws, and soft feathers for silent flying. Then ask children to pretend they are wise owls chosen to teach others about their kind. Have them write a fact-filled outline for their lesson. When children are ready to present the lesson, invite them to use their owl hand puppets to help teach it.

Nonfiction Literature Links

All About Owls
by Jim Arnosky
(Scholastic, 1995).
Naturalist Jim Arnosky observes owls and then answers his own questions about these amazing birds, using illustrations to bring their world to life.

Those Outrageous Owls
by Laura Wyatt
(Pineapple Press, 2006).
How do owls fly so quietly? Where do owls sleep? This photo-illustrated book answers these questions and more.

Head

4 Fold the 6- by 15-inch white paper in half the short way. Cut fringes, as shown, cutting through both layers. Unfold the paper.

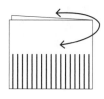

5 Color and cut out the eyes. Apply glue to the back center of the eyes and then attach them to the fringed white paper, as shown.

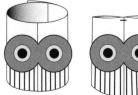

6 Overlap the ends of the fringed paper to form a tube-shaped head that's large enough to fit over the top of the body. Pinch the top closed and staple once in the middle, as shown.

7 Fold the brown square in half diagonally and place it as shown. Make a beak by folding up only the top layer of the lower corner. Then fold up the two top corners to create ear tufts. Line up the straight edge between the ear tufts with the top of the head. Then staple once in the center to hold the pieces together.

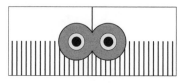

8 To keep the parts of the puppet together when not in use, tape one end of the yarn to the inside of the head and the other to the inside of the body.

9 To use, slide your hand through the body and into the head, poking your fingers through the top openings in the head. Then rotate your wrist to make the owl's head turn.

Now, your owl is ready to look around for its prey.

Mouse-in-Hiding

When winter winds blow, field mice seek shelter indoors. As this house-shaped card is opened, a cute but uninvited houseguest pops out in surprise—caught in the act of stealing a nice big chunk of cheese!

Materials

For each child:

- mouse patterns (page 67)
- 9- by 12-inch construction paper in a bright color (for card)
- construction paper scraps
- 9-inch square of brown construction paper

Other materials:

- scissors
- clear tape
- hole punch
- crayons or markers
- glue stick

Tip

Mice might have brown, gray, or white fur. Invite children to use their choice of these colors to make their mice.

What to Do

Make a copy of the mouse patterns for each child. Pass out the materials. Have children cut out the pattern box. Then demonstrate the following steps.

Card

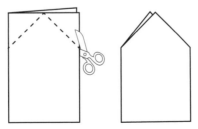

1 Fold the bright-colored paper in half the short way. Cut away the top corners to form a peaked roof.

2 Cut out a door and windows from scraps of paper. Glue them to the front of the house-shaped card. Add details with crayons or markers.

Write About It!

Do children know that mice live on every continent except Antarctica? Or that young mice are called "kittens?" Read aloud the books listed below, or share other factual references about mice. Invite children to list the mouse facts they learn. Then ask them to write fill-in-the-blank paragraphs about mice. Have them exchange their papers with classmates and complete the paragraphs.

Nonfiction Literature Links

Mice
by Kevin J. Holmes
(Capstone Press, 1998).
Full-page photos accompany this informative text about mice habitats, diet, enemies, senses, and their young.

Of Mice and Rats
by Allan Fowler
(Children's Press, 1998).
The life of mice is described through simple text and photos.

Mouse

3 Fold the brown square in half. Tape the mouse patterns to the paper along the fold, as shown. Cut out the head and body through both layers. Then punch a hole where indicated through both layers of the folded head.

4 Unfold the head. Color the tip of the mouse's nose. Then fold the ears forward, as shown. Refold the head.

5 Apply glue to the back of the right ear and along the right edge of the body. Open the card and position the pieces on the inside, as shown.

6 Apply glue to the other ear and along the left edge of the body. Close the card and press firmly so that the pieces adhere to the inside of the card. When you open the card, the mouse's nose and paws will pop out at you.

7 Cut a tail from brown scrap paper and glue it in place. Cut out a mouse hole from black scrap paper. Glue it to the opposite side of the card.

8 To give the mouse a chunk of cheese to hold, carefully cut apart the front paws at the fold. Cut a triangle from yellow scrap paper (punch holes in it for Swiss cheese.) Apply glue to the back of each paw, place the cheese between the paws, close the card, and press firmly.

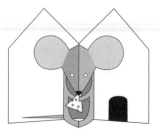

Now when you open the card, the mouse will appear to be taking a bite out of the cheese!

Migrating Monarch
page 8

Courageous Crow
page 10

Bat Hat
page 13

Masked Raccoon
page 15

Turkey Topper
page 18

Snooze-and-Wake
Bear
page 21

Playful Penguin
page 24

Snowshoe Hare
page 27

Observant Owl
page 29

Mouse-in-Hiding
page 31

Spring Lamb
page 33

Bobbin' Robin
page 36

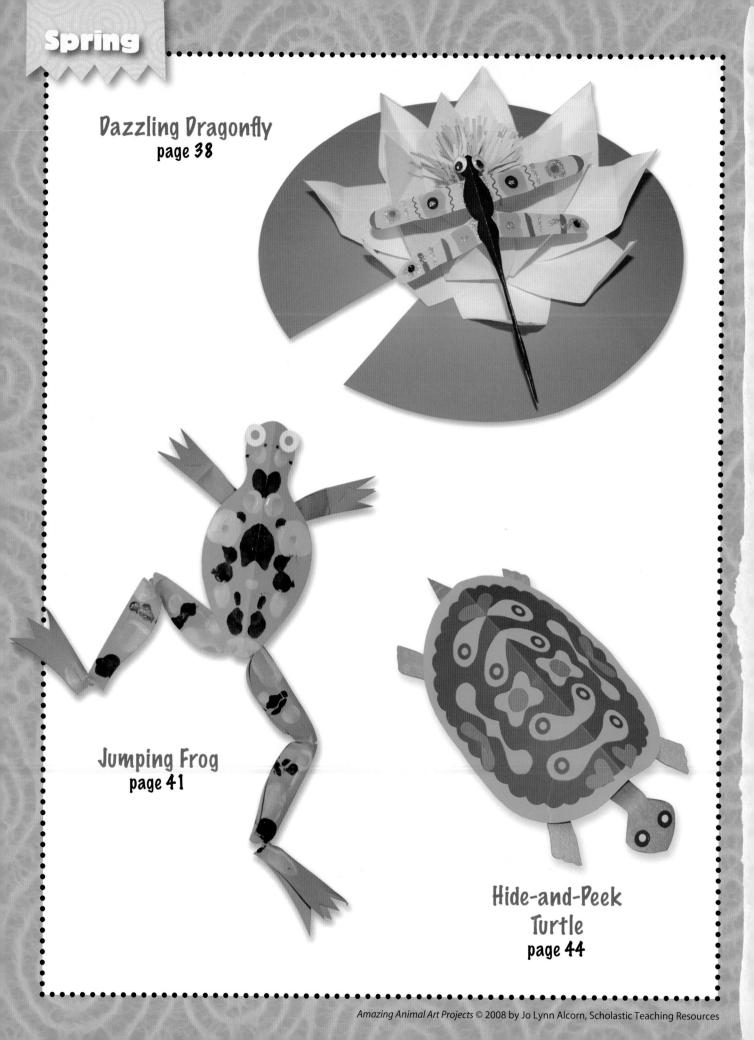

Dazzling Dragonfly
page 38

Jumping Frog
page 41

**Hide-and-Peek
Turtle**
page 44

Fish Mobile
page 47

Tropical Treetop
Toucan
page 49

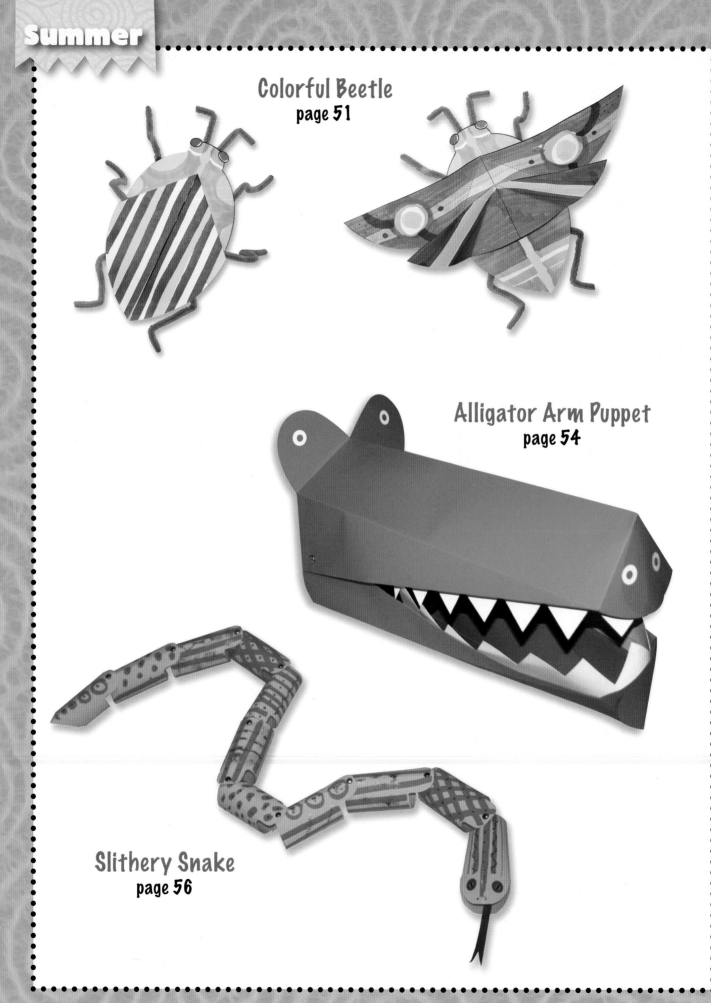

Colorful Beetle
page 51

Alligator Arm Puppet
page 54

Slithery Snake
page 56

Spring Lamb

In early spring, ewes give birth to their lambs, wobbly little bundles of wool that can barely stand. This adorable, woolly-looking paper lamb has legs and ears that children can move and pose into different positions.

Materials

For each child:

- lamb patterns (page 68)
- 8- inch square of black construction paper
- 2 hole reinforcements
- scrap of pink paper (for nose)
- three 4- by 6 ½-inch white sheets of construction paper
- 4 paper fasteners
- 9- by 12-inch white construction paper
- 1- by 10-inch posterboard (any color)
- two 2- by 12-inch sheets of black construction paper

Other materials:

- scissors
- clear tape
- hole punch
- glue stick

Tip

Lambs come in many different shades and combinations of black, white, and brown. Provide paper in different colors for children to choose from when making their lambs.

What to Do

Make a copy of the patterns for each child. Pass out the materials. Have children cut out the pattern boxes. Then demonstrate the following steps.

Head

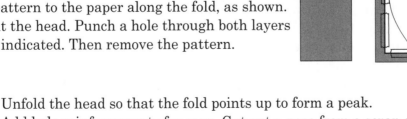

1 Fold the black square in half. Tape the head pattern to the paper along the fold, as shown. Cut out the head. Punch a hole through both layers where indicated. Then remove the pattern.

2 Unfold the head so that the fold points up to form a peak. Add hole reinforcements for eyes. Cut out a nose from a scrap of pink paper and glue it on the head.

Ears

3 Stack two of the 4- by 6 ½-inch pieces of white paper. Tape the ear pattern to the top paper, as shown. Cutting through both layers of paper, cut out the ears and punch holes where indicated. Separate the ears.

4 Line up the holes in one ear with the hole on one side of the head, sandwiching the head between the two holes in the ear. To attach the ear, push a paper fastener through the holes and flatten the prongs in the back. Repeat to attach the other ear. Move the hinged ears up and down a few times to make sure they can be moved with ease.

5 Cut out a cloud shape from the last 4- by 6 ½-inch white paper. Tape the shape to the top back of the head to resemble a tuft of wool, as shown.

Body

6 For the body, cut a large cloud shape from the 9- by 12-inch white paper. Punch two holes at the bottom of the body. Then tape the posterboard strip to the back of the body, as shown, to make a neck. Fold back the top one inch of the neck to form a tab.

7 Tape the head to the neck tab, as shown.

Legs

8 Stack the two 2- by 12-inch pieces of black paper. Round off the corners on one end, cutting through both layers. Then punch a hole at the other end, as shown.

9 Turn the lamb faceup. Use paper fasteners to attach each leg to the back of the body, as shown. Flatten the prongs in the back. Then move the hinged legs from side to side a few times to make sure they can be moved with ease.

Move the ears and legs into different positions. Now your lamb is ready to try out its long, wobbly legs. Baaaa!

Write About It!

After sharing books about lambs (see below), help children create a lamb fact web on which to record the information they have learned. Then, working as a class or with partners, have them use the lamb facts to make up verses to the tune of "Mary Had a Little Lamb" or another familiar tune. Invite them to use their moveable lambs as they sing the verses.

Nonfiction Literature Links

From Lamb to Sheep (How Do They Grow?) by Jillian Powell (Raintree, 2001). Easy-to-read text and photos describe how lambs grow into adult sheep.

Sheep (Early Reader Science) by Peter Brady and William Munoz (Bridgestone Books, 1996). This book introduces children to the role sheep play on a farm.

How to Display

Have children fringe sheets of green construction paper to make grass. Staple the paper grass to a bulletin board, overlapping the edges to create a green meadow. Then add the lambs, attaching them to the scene at the shoulders so their heads and legs can be moved. For a finishing touch, invite children to cut out flowers and clover to add to the meadow.

Bobbin' Robin

In the spring, robins return from their winter migration to build nests and lay eggs. When the eggs hatch, the parents work extra hard hunting for worms to feed their chirping, hungry nestlings. This diorama features a bobbin' red-breasted robin and a worm that tries to hide.

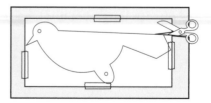

Materials

For each child:

* robin and worm patterns (pages 69–70)
* 6- by 12-inch white construction paper
* two 3- by 7-inch pieces of brown construction paper
* 12- by 18-inch green construction paper
* 2 paper fasteners

Other materials:

* scissors
* clear tape
* hole punch
* crayons
* stapler

Tip

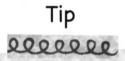

To give the wing more dimension, use one staple to fasten it to the body. Then pull the wing away from the body and ruffle the feathers.

What to Do

Make a copy of the patterns for each child. Pass out the materials. Have children cut out the pattern boxes. Then demonstrate the following steps.

Body and Wing

1 Tape the body pattern to the white paper and cut it out. Punch holes where indicated.

2 Use brown, red, and black crayons to color the robin's body. Be sure to color its chest red. Then add other details, such as a beak and tail feathers.

3 Tape the wing pattern along the top edge of a 3- by 7-inch piece of brown paper. Cut out and color the wing. Fringe the wing and then staple it to the body, as shown.

Worm

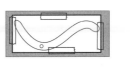

4 Tape the worm pattern to the remaining piece of brown paper. Cut out the worm and add details. Punch a hole where indicated.

Base

5 Fold the green paper in half the long way. Staple the open edges together. Fold the paper in half again. Then stand the paper on the table to form an L-shaped base. Punch a hole near the top edge of the base about 4 ½ inches away from each side, as shown.

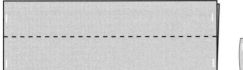

6 Use a paper fastener to attach the robin to one hole and the worm to the other.

Now your robin can go bobbin' for worms!

Variation

Replace the base with a brown paper nest. Add blue eggs that extend over the top of the nest. Then attach the robin to the nest.

Write About It!

The book *Where Robins Fly* (see below) opens with a page chock-full of action words, such as *dip, eat, flutter, feed, fly, poke, sing, sleep,* and *stretch*. Read the book aloud, pointing out the action words in the text (or read another book about robins and generate a new list of action words). Children might also generate a list of descriptive words about robins. Have children write an informative paragraph about robins, using as many action words from the list as possible. Their paragraphs might describe behaviors or specific actions of robins, such as feeding, bathing, and nest building.

Nonfiction Literature Links

A Nest Full of Eggs by Priscilla Belz Jenkins (HarperCollins, 1995). This illustrated book uses simple text to describe how robins prepare a nest for laying eggs and care for the baby birds that hatch.

Where Robins Fly by Anita Holmes (Benchmark Books, 2000). Vivid photos accompany simple but informative text about robins.

Dazzling Dragonfly

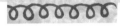

The shimmering, colorful dragonfly is a fast and powerful flier. It flits around the pond using its big eyes and sharp vision to find bugs to eat. This dazzling dragonfly alights on a lily pad and its lovely flower.

Materials

For each child:

- dragonfly and lily patterns (page 71)
- 4- by 8-inch white or bright-colored construction paper
- 2 wiggle eyes
- 12-inch square of green construction paper
- eight 3- by 6-inch pieces of white construction paper
- eight 3- by 4 ½-inch pieces of pink construction paper
- paper fastener
- 3- by 9-inch strip of yellow paper

Other materials:

- scissors
- markers, crayons, or paint
- glitter glue
- white glue
- clear tape
- hole punch

Tip

If desired, work with small groups to help children make their projects. Each child might make a dragonfly and then work with several other children to make one lily pad.

What to Do

Make a copy of the patterns for each child. Pass out the materials. Have children cut out the pattern boxes. Then demonstrate the following steps.

Dragonfly

1 Fold the 4- by 8-inch paper in half the short way. Turn the paper so that the open ends face away from you. Make a *V* with your first two fingers and place them on the fold, as shown. Trace around your fingers. Cut out the shape through both layers of paper, making sure not to cut the *V* in two between the fingers.

2 Open the *V*-shaped cutout, or wings. Decorate both sides of the wings with markers, crayons, or paint. Use glitter glue to add a dazzling effect to the wings.

3 Carefully cut out the body. Glue it to the wings, as shown. Then glue on the wiggle eyes. Allow the glue to dry.

Lily Pad and Flower

4 Round out the corners of the green paper. Cut a notch out of the paper to create a lily pad.

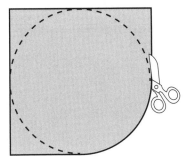

5 Stack two 3- by 6-inch pieces of white paper. Tape the large petal pattern to the top sheet. Cut out the petal, cutting through all layers. Repeat three times to create eight large petals. Punch a hole in each petal where indicated.

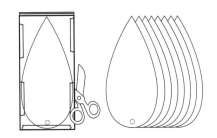

6 Repeat step 5 using the eight 3- by 4 ½-inch pieces of pink paper and the small petal pattern. To assemble the lily, stack the small petals on top of the large petals, push a paper fastener through the holes, and flatten the prongs in the back.

7 Spread out all the petals to create a flower. Then fold up the tip of each petal, as shown.

8 To make the stamen, fringe the yellow strip of paper. Apply a thin line of glue along the long uncut edge and roll the strip into a tube. Fit the tube upright over the head of the paper fastener and glue it in place. After the glue dries, spread apart and fold the fringed ends outward. Glue the flower to the lily pad.

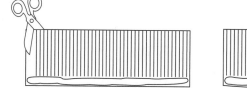

Now set your dragonfly on the lily pad where it can wait for yummy bugs to come along. But Mr. Dragonfly, beware of frogs!

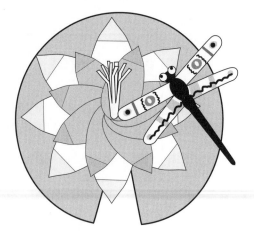

How to Display

Arrange a length of blue fabric on the floor to create a pond. Then place the lily pads and dragonflies on it. To give the scene more life, invite children to make the "Jumping Frog" (page 41) and "Hide-and-Peek Turtle" (page 44) to add to the pond.

Jumping Frog

In the spring, the chorus of croaks and ribbits coming from the pond announce that frogs have emerged from their winter hibernation. These amphibians, equally at home in water or on land, are strong swimmers and powerful jumpers. This paper frog features springy back legs and symmetrical markings that aid in camouflage.

Materials

For each child:

- frog patterns (page 72)
- 4- by 7-inch green construction paper
- three 3- by 9-inch pieces of green construction paper
- 2 hole reinforcements
- three 12-inch pipe cleaners

Other materials:

- scissors
- clear tape
- green and yellow tempera paint
- craft sticks
- stapler

Tip

For a less messy alternative to paint, have children use crayons or markers to create the symmetrical markings on the frog.

What to Do

Make a copy of the patterns for each child. Pass out the materials. Have children cut out the pattern boxes. Then demonstrate the following steps.

Body

1 Fold the 4- by 7-inch paper in half the long way. Tape the body pattern to the paper along the fold. Cut out the body and unfold it.

2 To make a symmetrical design on the frog, use a craft stick to apply dots of paint to one side of the inside of the body. While the paint is still wet, fold the body, rub gently, and unfold it. Allow the paint to dry. Add hole reinforcements for eyes. Then fold the unpainted sides of the body toward each other to create a ridge along the frog's back.

Legs

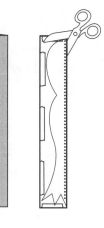

3 Fold a 3- by 9-inch green paper in half the long way. Tape the back leg pattern to the paper along the fold. Cut out the back leg. Repeat to cut out the other back leg. If desired, create a symmetrical design on each leg as described in step 2.

4 Place a pipe cleaner in the fold of each back leg, as shown. Fold and staple along the length of the leg, stapling close to the pipe cleaner to keep it in place. Also, staple each foot closed.

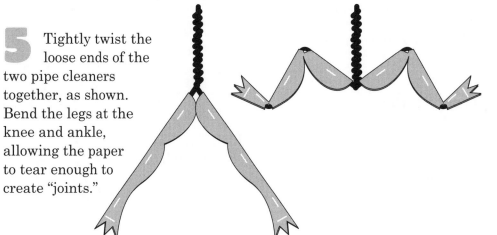

5 Tightly twist the loose ends of the two pipe cleaners together, as shown. Bend the legs at the knee and ankle, allowing the paper to tear enough to create "joints."

6 Fold the remaining 3- by 9-inch green paper in half the long way. Tape the pattern for the front legs to the paper along the fold. Cut out and unfold the front legs.

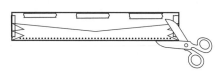

7 Bend the remaining pipe cleaner in half. Place it in the fold of the front legs, as shown. Then fold and staple along the length of the front legs, stapling close to the pipe cleaner to keep it in place. Also, staple the foot on each end closed. Gently bend the front legs to form a *V*. Fold the feet upward.

8 Place the front legs, feet pointing up, above the back legs. Then wrap the loose end of the pipe cleaner once around the front legs, as shown, to hold them in place.

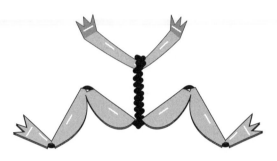

9 Place the frog's body, painted side facedown, on the table. Flip the legs over and place on top of the body. Tape the pipe-cleaner "backbone" securely to the body to attach the front and back legs.

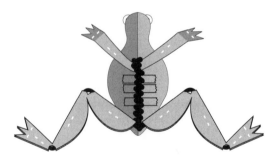

Turn your frog over and he's ready to hop away!

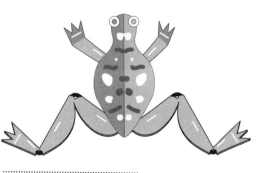

Write About It!

Frogs are fabulous jumpers, swimmers, and insect-eaters. Have children research and share fun facts about frogs performing each of the three activities. Then ask them to write similes or metaphors that describe these particular actions of this fantastic critter.

Nonfiction Literature Links

All About Frogs by Jim Arnosky (Scholastic, 2002). This author/illustrator's acrylic illustrations beautifully complement the informative text that delves into all aspects of a frog's life.

Amazing Frogs and Toads (Dorling Kindersley, 1990). This book is packed with information. Each spread is organized to highlight a particular theme, such as curious colors or a big appetite. Each fact is supported with a photo or illustration.

How to Display

To display, children can bend their frogs' back legs in different positions. If you made the pond for "Dazzling Dragonfly" (see page 40), invite children to tuck their frogs under and around the lily pads, poised to nab a dragonfly lunch.

Hide-and-Peek Turtle

Turtles are slow moving reptiles with hard shells that protect them from predators. This paper turtle sticks out its head to warm it in the sun, and then ducks into its shell whenever it feels shy—which is often!

Materials

For each child:

❀ turtle pattern (page 73)

❀ 8- by 14-inch white posterboard

❀ 2 hole reinforcements

❀ two 8- by 9-inch sheets of different colored construction paper

❀ construction paper scraps

Other materials:

❀ scissors

❀ glue stick

❀ stapler

❀ crayons or markers

Tip

To make tracing the patterns easier for younger children, create one-piece tagboard templates that incorporate the head- and tail-ends of the turtle.

What to Do

Make a copy of the pattern for each child. Pass out the materials. Have children cut out the pattern. Then demonstrate the following steps.

Body

1 Place the pattern on the posterboard so that the turtle's head touches one end, as shown. Use a crayon to trace the pattern.

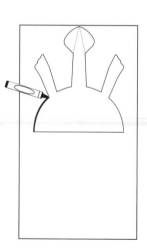

2 Remove the pattern. Cut along the dotted lines to make a pattern for the tail end of the turtle.

44

3 Place the pattern on the posterboard, lining up the straight edge with the straight line of the turtle outline. The tail should point to the end of the posterboard. Trace the pattern.

4 Cut out the turtle and color its head, legs, and tail. Attach hole reinforcements for eyes.

Shell

5 Stack and fold the two 8- by 9-inch papers in half the long way. Use scissors to round off the outer corners, as shown.

6 Separate the two folded shapes. Set one aside to use as the shell base. For the shell topper, cut away about ½ inch from the curved edge of the other folded shape. Fold that shape in half again. Then use a pencil to draw a few shapes that start and end at the folded edges, as shown. Cut out the shapes.

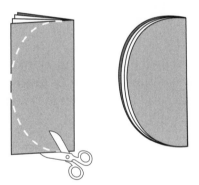

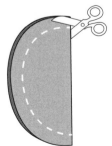

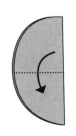

7 Unfold the shell topper and base. Center and glue the topper onto the base. If desired, cut out small shapes from scrap paper. Add these to the shell to create more detail and color.

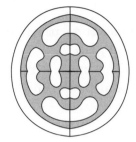

8 Place the shell facedown. Then position the body facedown on top of and near the left edge of the shell, as shown. Staple the body in place. Then push the right edge of the shell inward to meet the body and staple it in place. When you turn the turtle over, the shell will form a dome over its body.

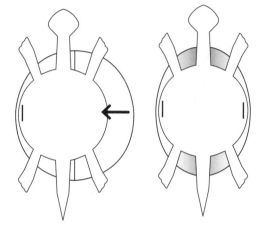

Tip

To give the turtle more dimension, bend the legs and tail down slightly away from the shell.

9 Turn the turtle faceup. To make the turtle draw in its head, gently push the head straight back to wedge it inside the shell.

If your turtle feels shy, push its head into the shell. Then pull its head out when the turtle's ready to look around.

How to Display

If you made the pond for "Dazzling Dragonfly" (see page 40), invite children to add their turtles to the display, placing them in the pond and around its edges.

Fish Mobile

The underwater world of fish is full of variety and color. For protection, small fish often swim close together in groups, or schools, so they appear to be one large fish. The fish in this mobile move in a school—they all swim in the same direction and dart away together when danger appears!

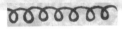

Materials

For each child:

❀ fish pattern (page 74)

For each mobile:

❀ four 12-inch pipe cleaners

❀ 24-inch length of yarn

Other materials:

❀ crayons and markers

❀ glitter glue

❀ scissors

❀ glue stick

Tip

eeeeee

For best results, use twelve fish on a single mobile. If desired, have children make several fish each to add to the mobiles.

ᘘᘘᘘᘘᘘᘘᘘ

What to Do

Make a copy of the pattern for each child. Pass out the materials. Then demonstrate the following steps.

Fish

1 Use crayons, markers, and glitter glue to decorate a fish pattern, creating a mirror image on the two sides of the fish.

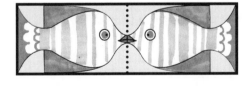

2 Fold the fish pattern in half on the dotted line. Cut out the fish, cutting through both layers.

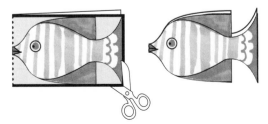

Write About It!

The books listed below provide a great springboard for writing poems about fish. Use the colors, patterns, and fascinating features of the fish in these books to inspire children to write descriptive poetry about the creatures of the deep blue sea. To help get children started, you might model a variety of poetry formats, from couplets to free verse.

Nonfiction Literature Links

Fish Faces
by Norbert Wu
(Henry Holt and Company, 1997).
Celebrate fish through the rhythmic text and breathtaking photos of this inspiring book.

Hello, Fish!:
Visiting the Coral Reef
by Sylvia A. Earle
(National Geographic Society, 1999).
A marine biologist introduces readers to twelve fascinating fish—each presented with lines of poetry, informative text, and a full-page photo.

Mobile

3 Decide how many fish you want to use to make a mobile. Then decide how many will be displayed on each of the three pipe cleaners that will be used to hold the fish (four fish per pipe cleaner work well). Collect the fish from children.

4 Unfold each fish and apply glue to one side of the inside. Then fold the two sides of the fish together, trapping the pipe cleaner between the sides, as shown. Attach the first fish to the bottom of each pipe cleaner and work upward to add others. Leave the top three inches of each pipe cleaner free.

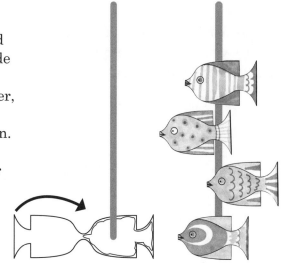

5 To make the top support bar of the mobile, bend the ends of the fourth pipe cleaner to form a hook at each end. Then loop the top end of a fish-filled pipe cleaner through each hook and bend the tip to keep it in place. Hook the last fish-filled pipe cleaner over the center of the top support bar. To make a hanger, tie one end of the yarn to the center of the mobile. Then suspend the mobile so that it moves freely.

Gently blow on the mobile to make the school of fish swim about!

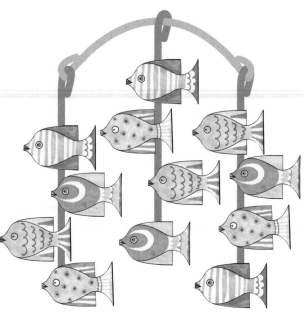

Tropical Treetop Toucan

The noisy toucan has a huge, colorful bill and lives in the heat of the tropics. Children can wear this exotic-looking hat as they imagine what it's like to be a toucan sitting in the treetops of the rainforest!

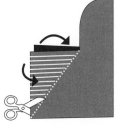

Materials

For each child:

* toucan patterns (pages 75–76)
* 12- by 18-inch black construction paper
* 6- by 9-inch yellow construction paper
* 2 hole reinforcements
* 2- by 24-inch strip of black posterboard
* 9- by 12-inch brightly colored construction paper (for tail)

Other materials:

* scissors
* clear tape
* color markers
* glue stick
* stapler
* white crayon

Tip

For a more realistic toucan, have children paint the neck and chest of their bird with yellow or white tempera paint. They might also make a black tail and then paint the underside of its base red or orange.

What to Do

Make a copy of the patterns for each child. Pass out the materials. Have children cut out the pattern boxes. Then demonstrate the following steps.

Body

1 Fold the black paper in half the short way. Tape the body pattern to the paper along the fold, as shown. Cut out the gray shape and discard it. Carefully remove the pattern and tape.

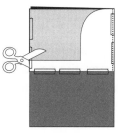

2 To make wings, fold each top corner of the paper out and toward the bottom, as shown. Unfold the wings and then fringe each one from the side edge to the fold.

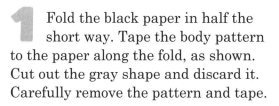

Write About It!

Why are toucans called the "clowns" of the tropical rain forest? How do they get water high up into their tree homes? Have children work with partners or in small groups to research toucans to find the answers, as well as to learn other information about these fascinating birds (such as what they eat, if they play, and how they communicate with each other). Ask them to write a paragraph or two about their findings and then illustrate their work. After sharing, you might compile the children's pages into a class book.

Nonfiction Literature Links

Toucans
by Lorien Kite
(Brown Partworks, 1999).
Full-page photos and clear, informative text organize information about toucans by topics.

Toucans
by Mary Ann McDonald
(Child's World, 2006).
The text of this book is clearly written, well organized, and supported with colorful, full-page photos featuring toucans.

3 Fold the yellow paper in half the long way. Tape the bill pattern along the fold, as shown. Cut out the bill, unfold it, and use the markers to decorate it with bold colors.

4 Place the bill facedown and apply glue along the short angled edges. Sandwich the top folded edge of the body between the two sides of the bill, as shown. Add hole reinforcements for eyes.

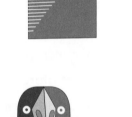
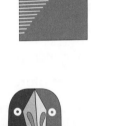

5 Pull back the top layer of the bill and add glue along the curved edge. Press the layer back in place.

6 Unfold the body. Center it in on top of the posterboard strip, as shown. Then staple the body to the strip to create a headband. Cover the staples on the back of the headband with tape.

Tail

7 Decorate the 9- by 12-inch paper. Accordion-fold the paper and staple the folds together at one end, as shown.

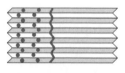

8 Help each child fit the headband around his or her head. Use the white crayon to mark where the two ends meet at the back. Sandwich the stapled end of the tail between the ends, lining up its edge with the marks. Staple the tail in place, as shown. Then trim the excess ends of the headband.

Now the toucan is ready for its head-top perch!

Colorful Beetle

With thousands of different species, beetles are one of the most numerous and varied creatures on earth. A beetle's hard outer shell is actually formed by a set of retractable wings that cover a second set of lower wings. Children will enjoy exploring pattern and color when they design their own unique beetles with this project.

Materials

For each child:

- beetle patterns (pages 77–78)
- three 12-inch lengths of black pipe cleaners
- 4-inch length of black pipe cleaner

Other materials:

- crayons
- scissors
- hole punch
- clear tape
- glue stick

Tip

To make the beetle sparkle, use glitter crayons or glitter glue to decorate the wings.

What to Do

Make a copy of the patterns for each child. Pass out the materials. Then demonstrate the following steps.

Body and Legs

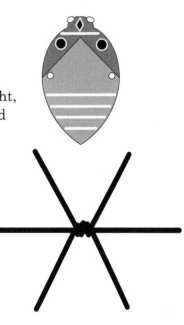

1 Color the body, using bold patterns and bright, contrasting colors. Then cut out the body and punch holes where indicated.

2 To make a set of legs, twist the three 12-inch-long pipe cleaners together at the center. Spread out the ends so that they resemble an *X* with a horizontal line through its middle, as shown.

51

Tip

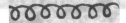

Bend back the tips of the pipe-cleaner antennae and legs to help prevent children from getting scratched by the pointed ends.

3 Working from the back of the body, poke the horizontal legs through the holes in the sides. Then, with the body faceup, bend each leg to form joints, as shown.

4 Turn the body facedown and tape the lower legs in place. Bend the 4-inch length of pipe cleaner to form antennae. Then tape the antennae in place on the back of the head, as shown.

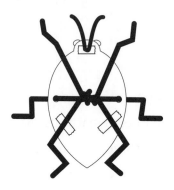

Wings

5 Color a bold, bright design on the left side of each upper wing pattern. Then create a mirror image of that design on the right side. Cut out the pattern, turn it facedown, and color a different mirror-image pattern on the back of each one, as shown. Repeat with the lower wing pattern. Turn the wings faceup when finished.

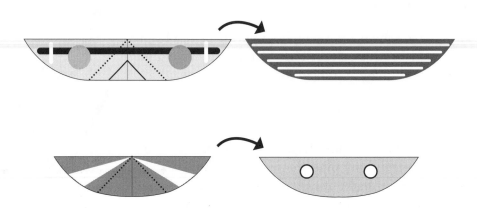

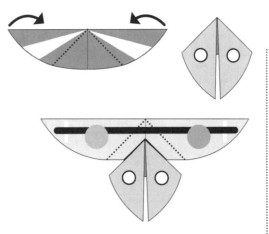

6 Fold down each corner of the lower wing along the dotted line. Then glue the lower wings to the upper wings, as shown, applying glue only to the small triangular area at the bottom of the upper wings.

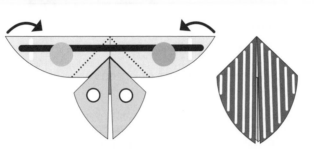

7 Fold down the corners of the upper wings along the dotted lines. The folded upper wings will cover the lower wings.

8 To attach the wings to the body, apply a wide line of glue just under the solid angled lines on the body. Then fit the pointed end of the folded upper wings along the lines and press the wings into place. Allow the glue to dry.

Lift and spread your beetle's wings and he'll be ready to fly away!

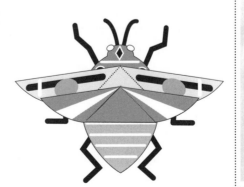

Nonfiction Literature Links

Beetles and Bugs: A Maurice Pledger Nature Trail Book by A. Wood (Silver Dolphin Books, 2003). Beautiful illustrations and informative text explore the fascinating world of beetles.

The Big Bug Book by Margery Facklam (Little, Brown, 1994). In addition to other bugs, this book highlights the Goliath beetle, Longhorn Harlequin beetle, and Hercules beetle. Each creature is featured on a spread, which includes in-depth information and actual-size illustrations.

Alligator Arm Puppet

Found only in the United States and China, alligators are cold-blooded reptiles that live in swamps and marshes. This paper gator features its characteristic long snout and king-size set of choppers! Children will love using this life-size arm puppet to share what they know about gators.

Materials

For each child:

- alligator pattern (page 79)
- two 12- by 18-inch sheets of green construction paper
- 4 hole reinforcements
- 3- by 18-inch white construction paper
- 2 paper fasteners

Other materials:

- scissors
- crayon
- clear tape
- glue stick
- hole punch

Tip

To make crisp, straight folds in step 3, help children score the paper by using a ruler and ball point pen to draw the fold lines before folding.

What to Do

Make a copy of the pattern for each child. Pass out the materials. Have children cut out the pattern. Then demonstrate the following steps.

Head

1 Fold a green paper in half the long way. Place the head pattern along the fold, as shown. Trace around the top edge, flip the pattern toward the other end, as shown, and trace again. Repeat with the other green paper. Cut out the shapes.

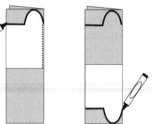

2 For the snout, unfold one of the papers and place it so that the fold faces down to form a valley. Fold the long straight edges toward the center fold, as shown.

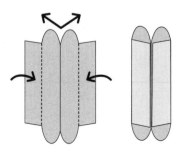

3 Unfold the snout, place it as shown, and fold the bottom corner of each side toward the center to create angled sides. Tape the corners in place.

4 Fold up the rounded tabs at the bottom end of the snout. Pull the tabs together to overlap them. Then glue them in place.

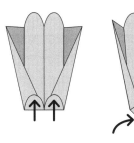

5 Turn the snout over. Fold up the other set of rounded tabs, as shown. For eyes, attach a hole reinforcement to each tab. Attach two hole reinforcements to the closed end to make nostrils.

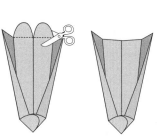

6 To make the jaw, repeat steps 2 through 4 with the other folded sheet of green paper. Cut off the second set of tabs.

Teeth

7 Fold the white paper in half the short way. Cutting through both layers, cut a zigzag line across the middle of the paper to form two sets of teeth. Glue one set to the inside of the snout and the other inside the jaw.

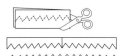

8 To assemble the gator, fit the snout over the jaw, as shown. Punch a hole through the overlapping section on each side. Then poke a paper fastener through each hole and flatten it in the back.

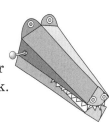

To make your gator chomp, slide one arm into the back of its mouth and the other arm under its jaw. Then move your arms to make its hinged mouth open and close. Chomp away!

Slithery Snake

It's summertime and scaly snakes are slithering all around! These legless reptiles use their tongues to taste, smell, and feel—and their eyes are always open! Children can make this easy-to-assemble, jointed viper to be as long as they'd like. Anaconda, anyone?

Materials

For each child:

* snake patterns (page 80)
* twelve 4 ½- by 6-inch pieces of construction paper in a bright color
* 2 hole reinforcements
* 11 paper fasteners
* scrap of red construction paper

Other materials:

* scissors
* clear tape
* hole punch
* markers or glitter glue

Tip

Invite children to use more or fewer body sections to make their snakes as long as they desire. To strengthen the snake's joints, have them cover each hole with a hole reinforcement before connecting the sections.

What to Do

Make a copy of the patterns for each child. Pass out the materials. Have children cut out the pattern boxes. Then demonstrate the following steps.

Head

1 Fold a 4 ½- by 6-inch piece of paper in half the short way. Tape the head pattern to the paper along the fold, as shown. Cutting through both layers, cut away the gray section of the pattern and discard it.

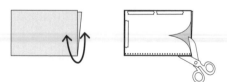

2 Unfold the head and use markers or glitter glue to decorate it. (If using glue, allow time for it to dry.) Add hole reinforcements for eyes. Punch a hole at the center along the long straight edge.

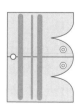

Body and Tail

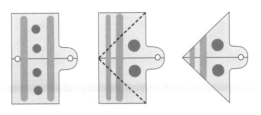

3 For each section of the body, repeat step 1 using a 4 ½- by 6-inch piece of paper and the body pattern. Unfold and decorate each section.

4 Punch a hole in the rounded tab on all the body sections. Then punch a hole at the center along the long straight edge of all but one body section. Cut off the corners of this section, as shown, to form a tail.

5 Use paper fasteners to connect the head, body sections, and tail, as shown. Place the tabbed end of each section on top at each connection.

6 Turn the snake facedown. Pull the two sides of the head together and overlap them to form a tube. Tape the ends in place. Repeat for each section and the tail.

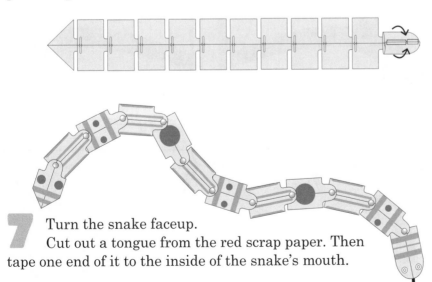

7 Turn the snake faceup.
Cut out a tongue from the red scrap paper. Then tape one end of it to the inside of the snake's mouth.

Slither away, snake!

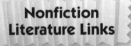

Write About It!

Slithering and sliding, striped and scaly, silently sneaking—and suddenly snatching! How many instances of alliteration can children use to write a snake poem? For added fun, have them write their poem inside a snake outline drawn on large construction paper. Or have children form the lines of their poem into the shape of a snake.

Nonfiction Literature Links

The Best Book of Snakes by Christiane Gunzi (Kingfisher, 2003). This beautifully illustrated book takes readers deep into the world of snakes, with topics covering warning signs, color and camouflage, how snakes move, and much more.

Snakes by Seymour Simon (HarperCollins, 1994). The author teams up with the Smithsonian Institution to present young readers with exceptional photos and text about this fascinating reptile.

Migrating Monarch

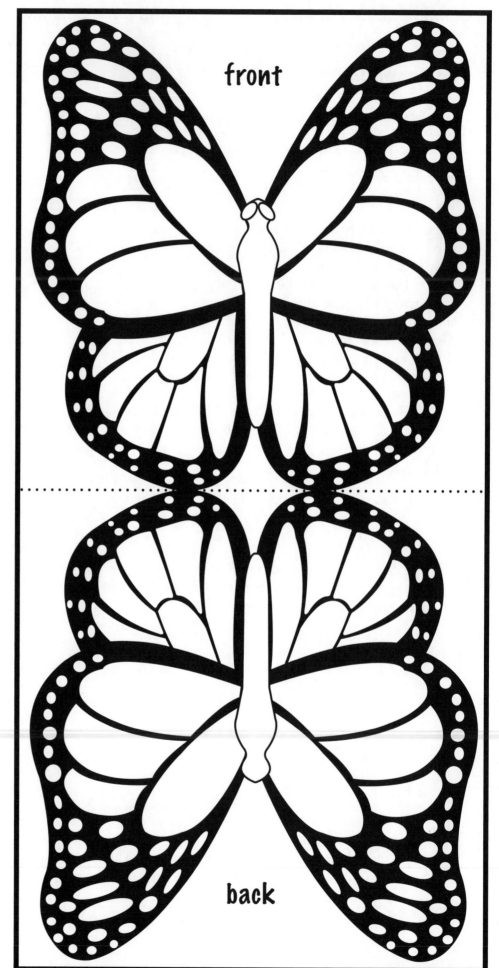

front

back

Amazing Animal Art Projects © 2008 by Jo Lynn Alcorn, Scholastic Teaching Resources

Courageous Crow

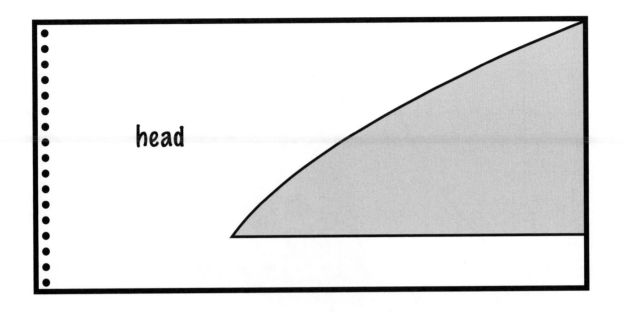

head

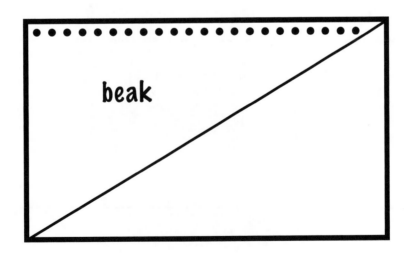

beak

Masked Raccoon

Fold.

right
paw

head

left
paw

Fold.

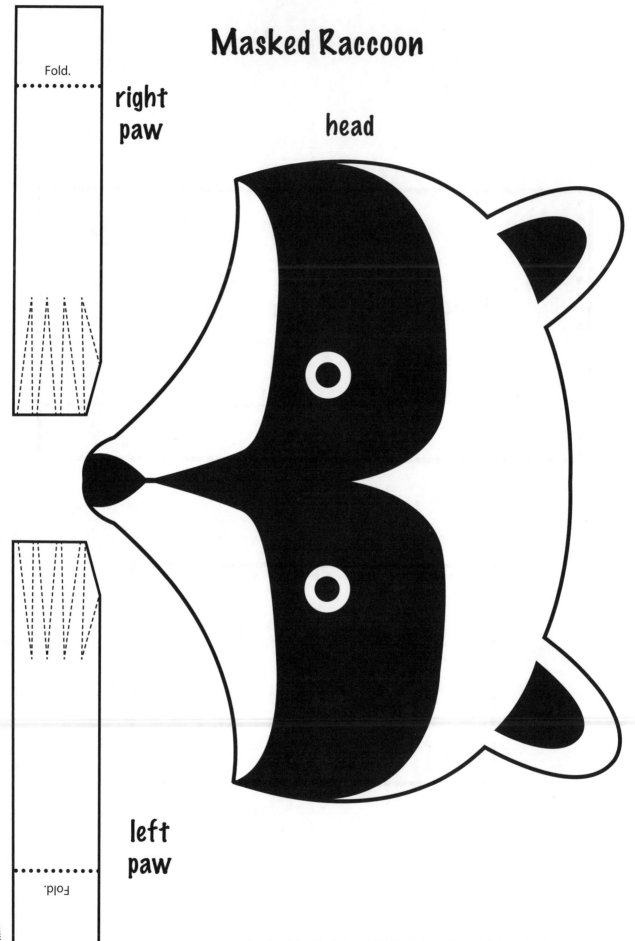

Turkey Topper

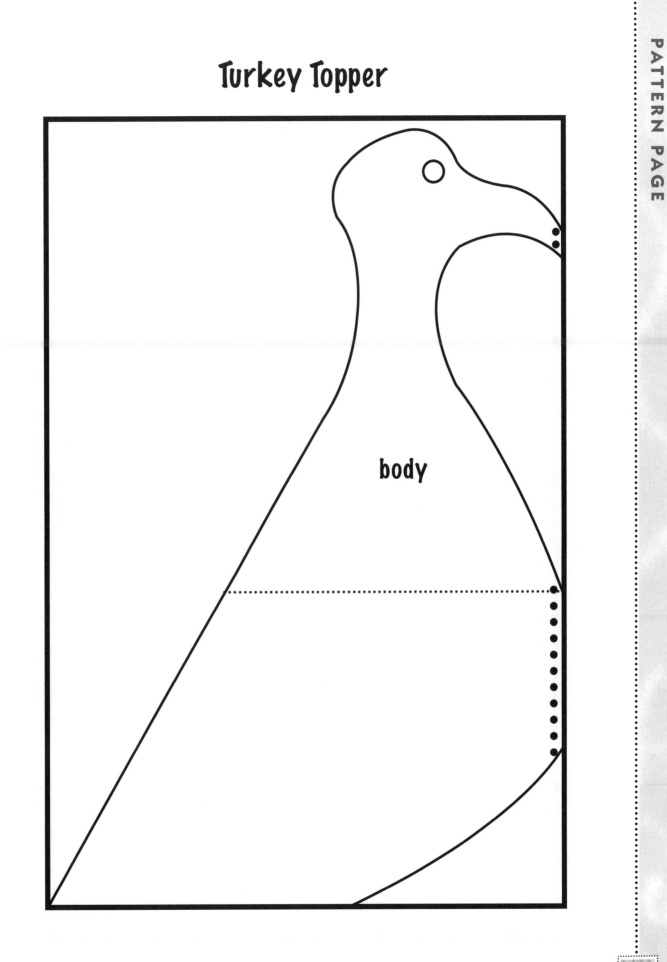

body

Snooze-and-Wake Bear

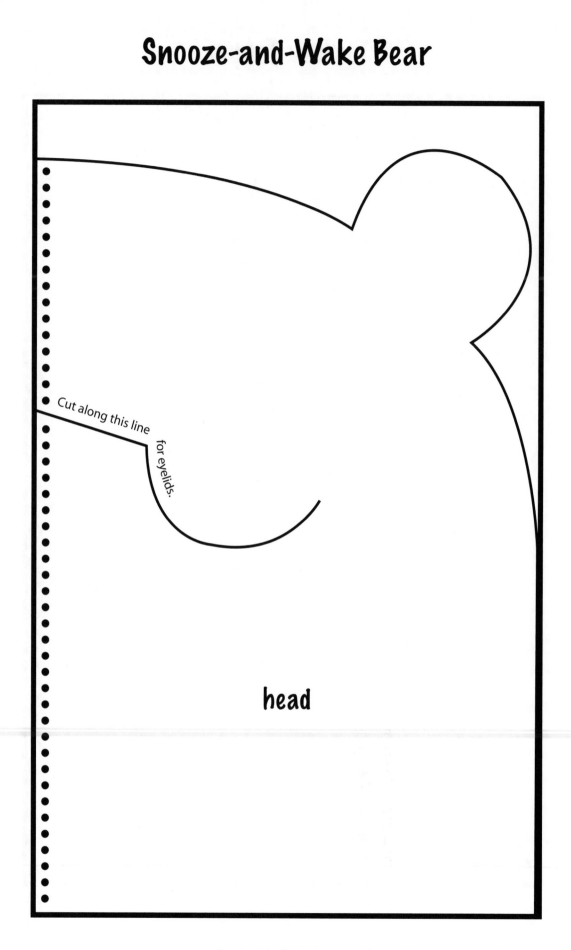

Cut along this line

for eyelids.

head

Amazing Animal Art Projects © 2008 by Jo Lynn Alcorn, Scholastic Teaching Resources

Snooze-and-Wake Bear

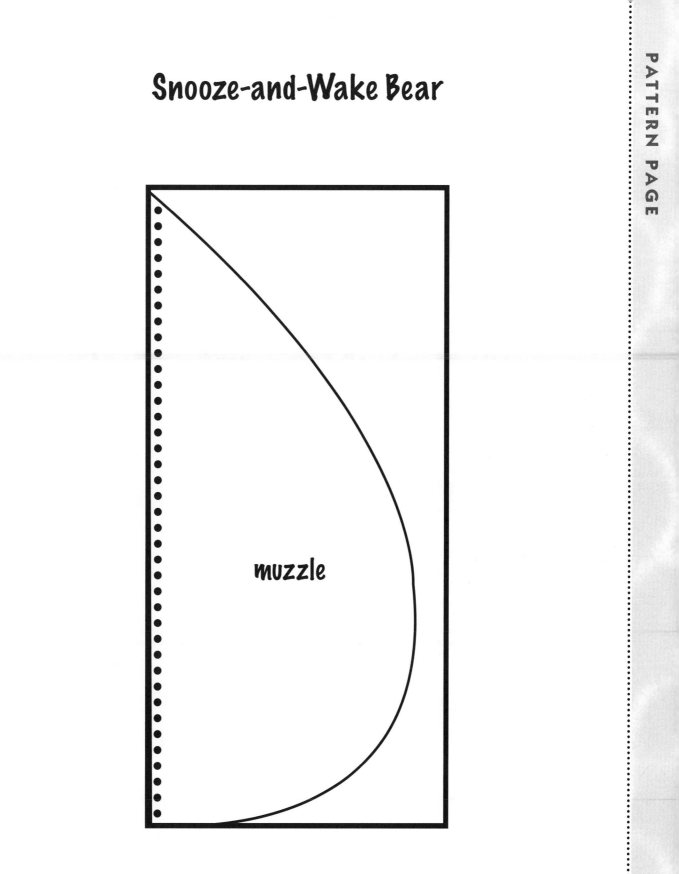

muzzle

Playful Penguin

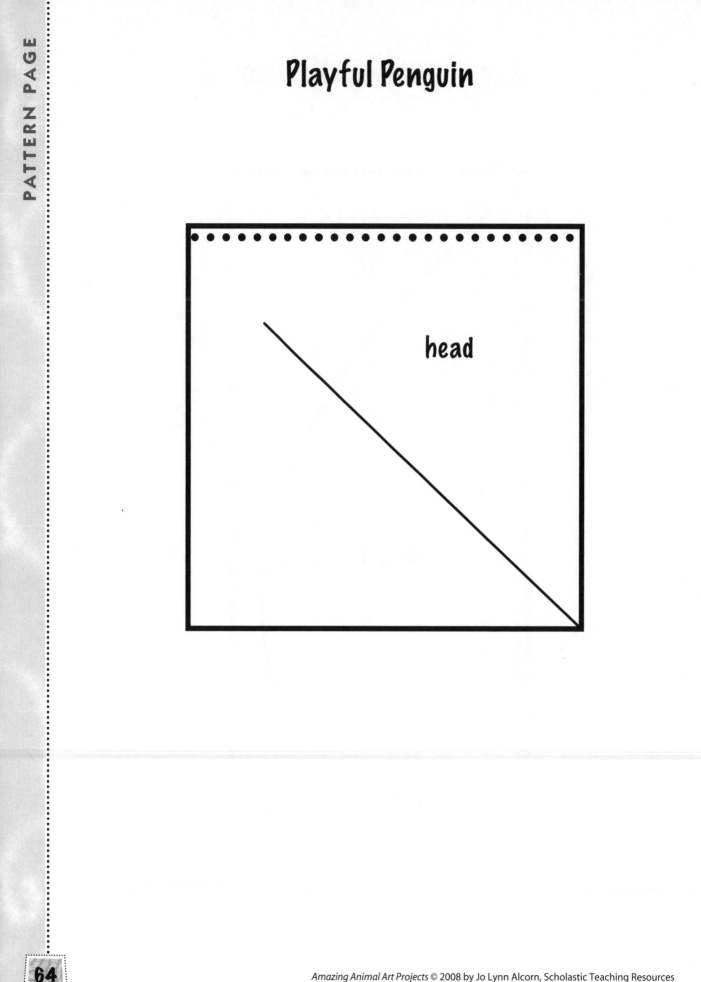

head

Snowshoe Hare

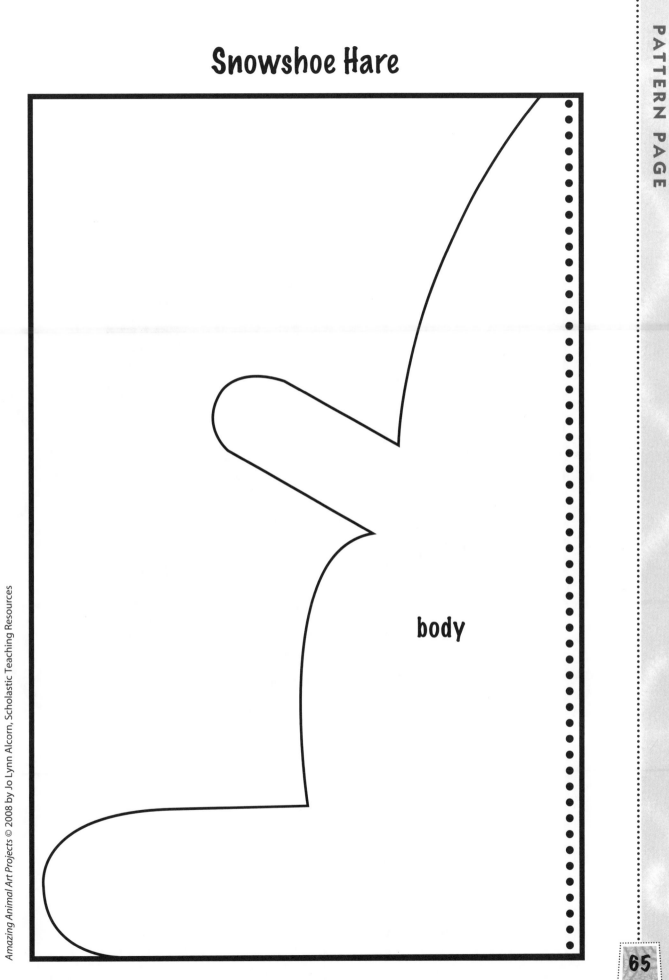

body

Snowshoe Hare

Observant Owl

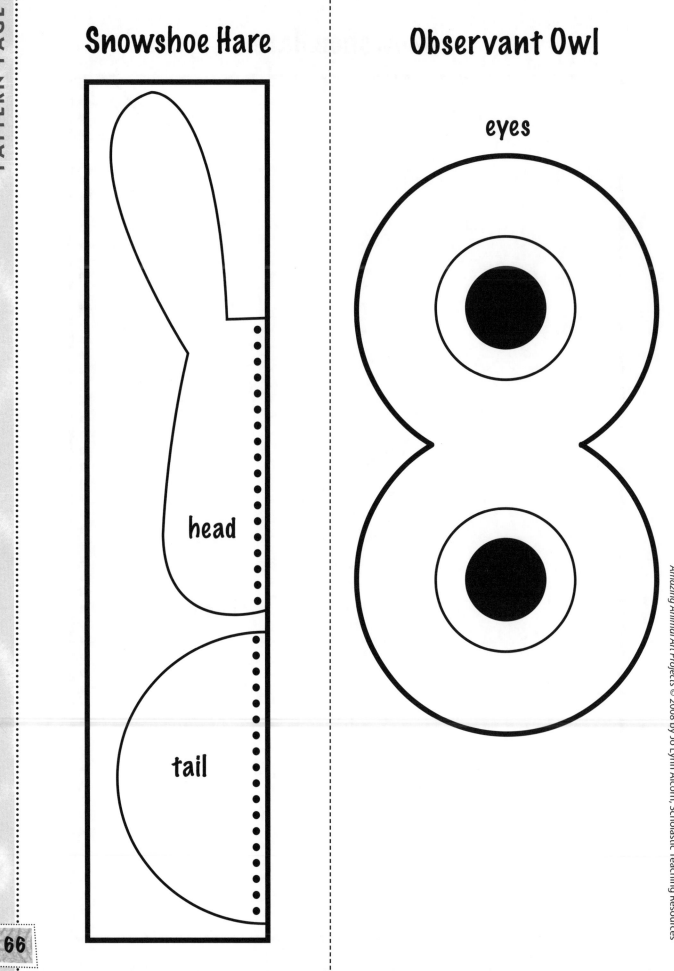

head

tail

eyes

Mouse -in -Hiding

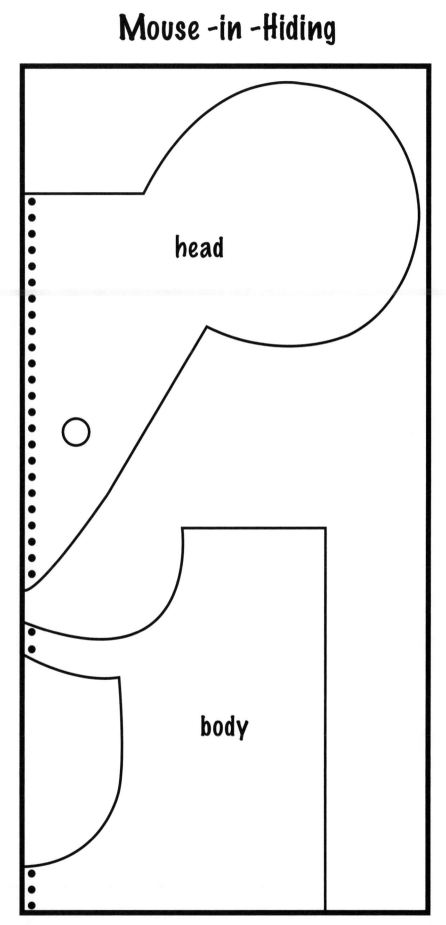

head

body

Spring Lamb

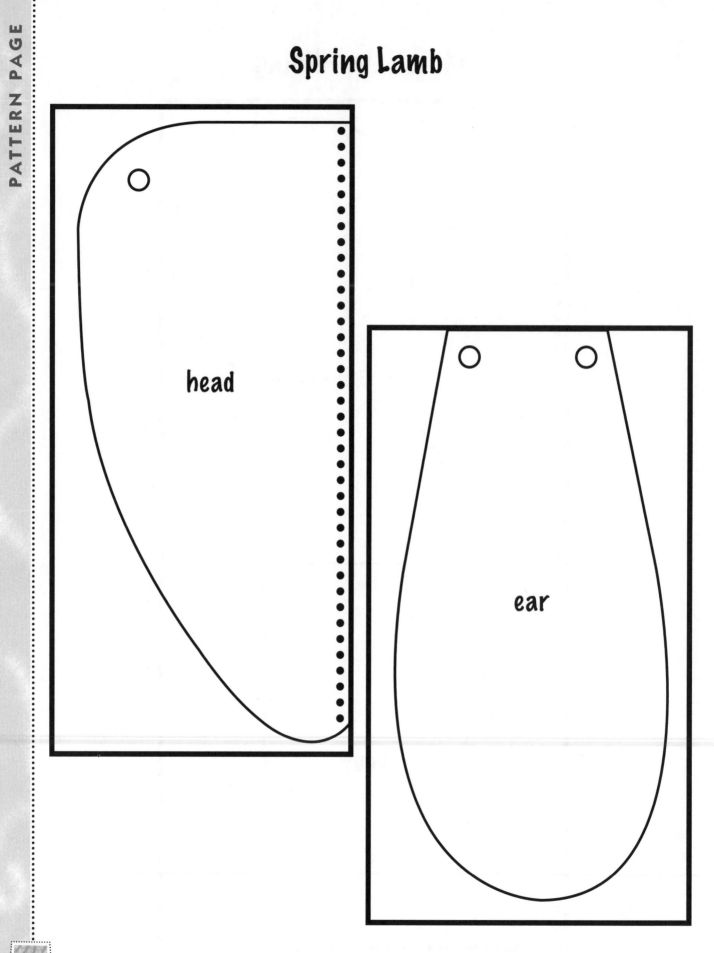

head

ear

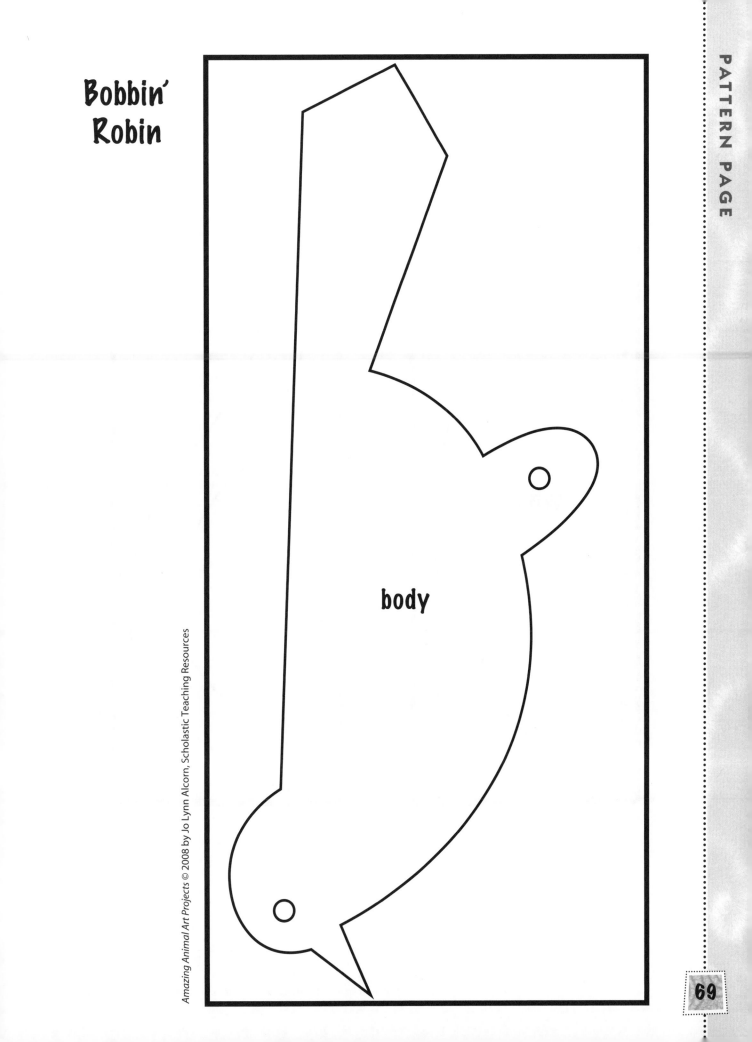

Bobbin'
Robin

body

Bobbin' Robin

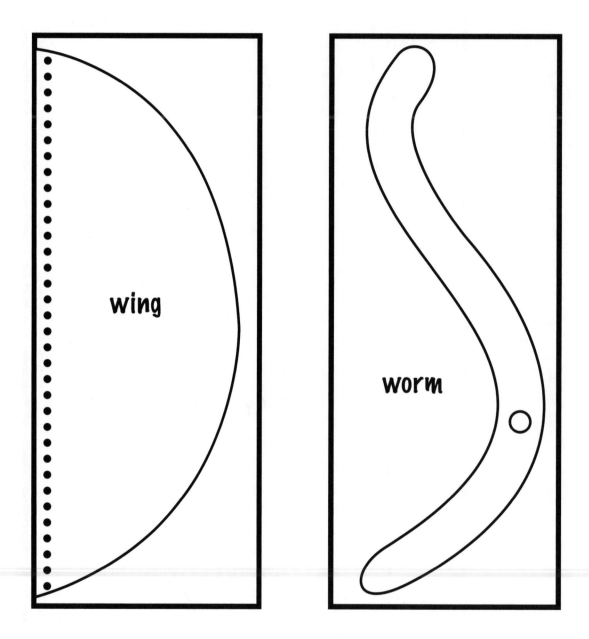

wing

worm

Amazing Animal Art Projects © 2008 by Jo Lynn Alcorn, Scholastic Teaching Resources

Dazzling Dragonfly

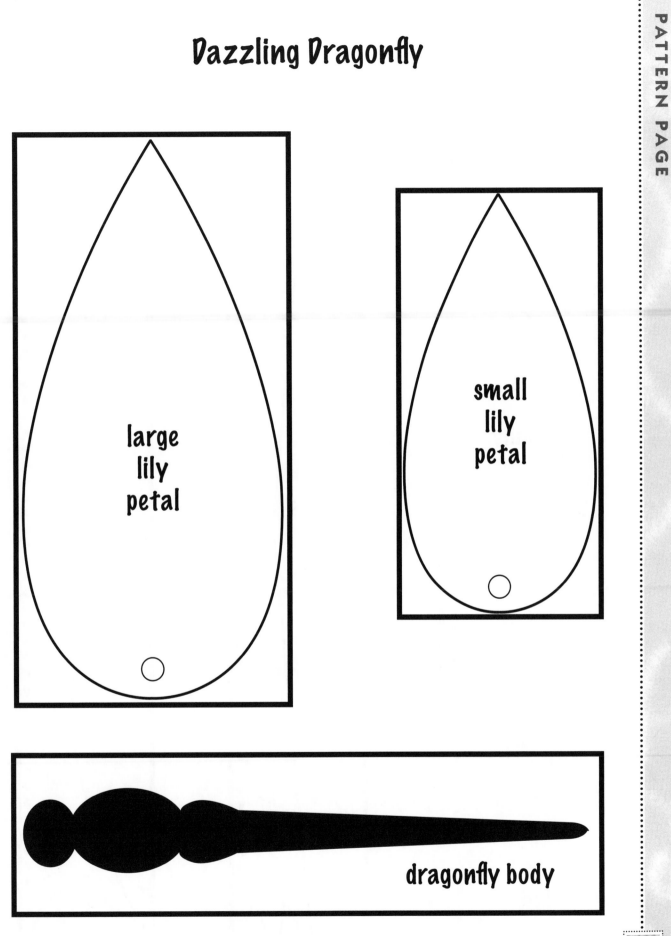

large
lily
petal

small
lily
petal

dragonfly body

Jumping Frog

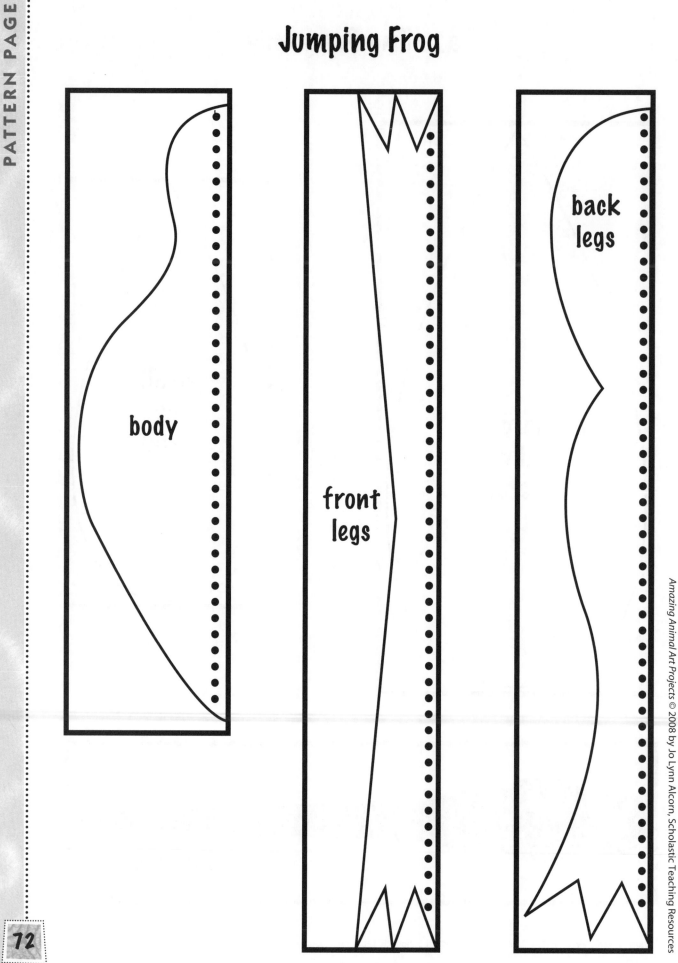

body

front
legs

back
legs

Hide-and-Peek Turtle

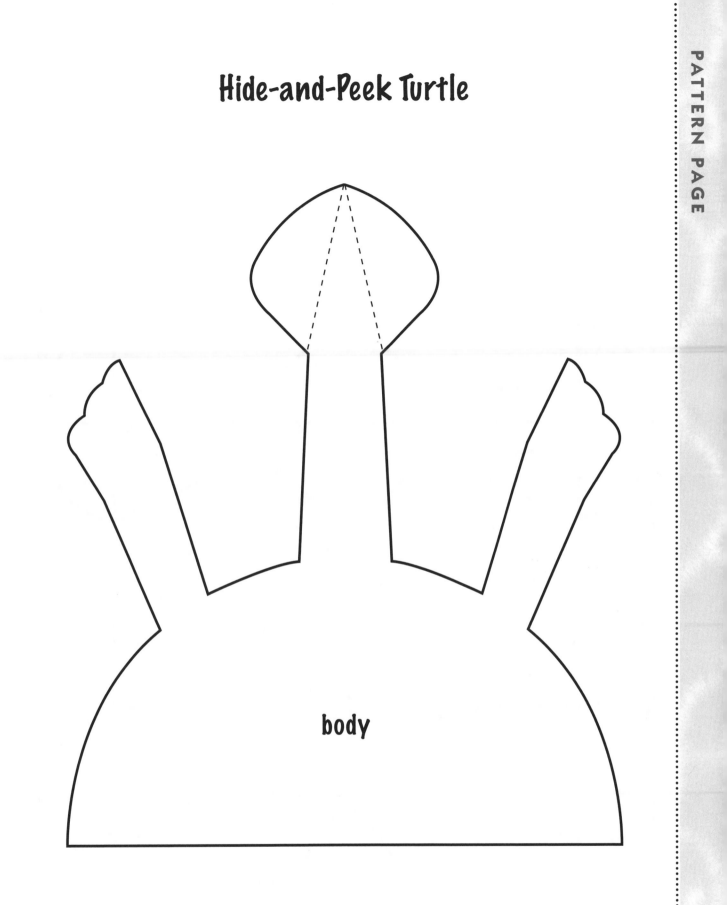

body

Fish Mobile

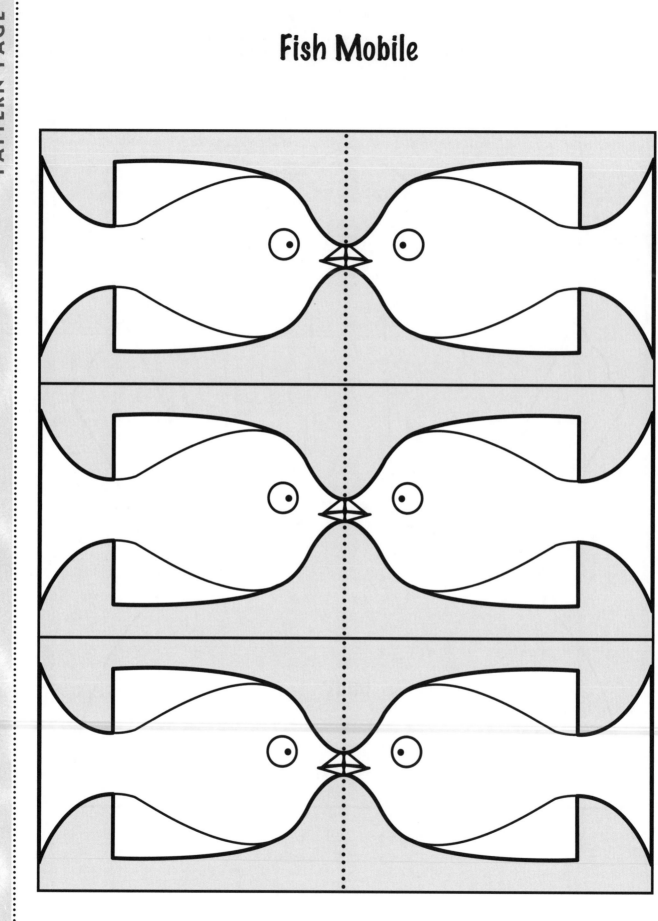

Tropical Treetop Toucan

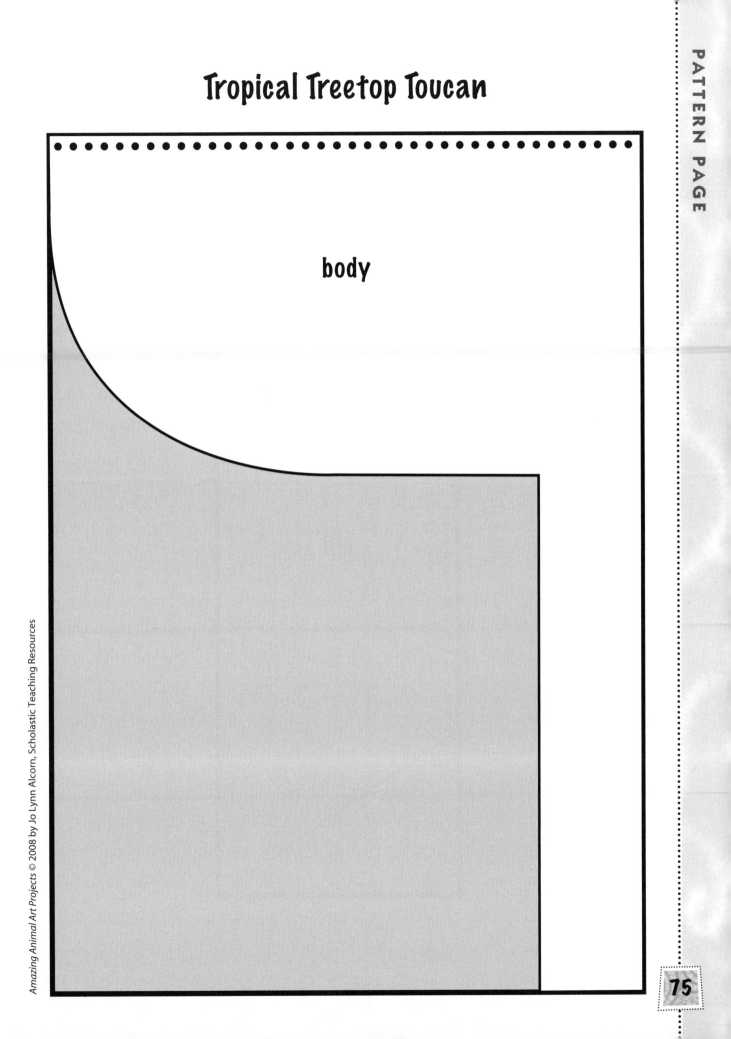

body

Tropical Treetop Toucan

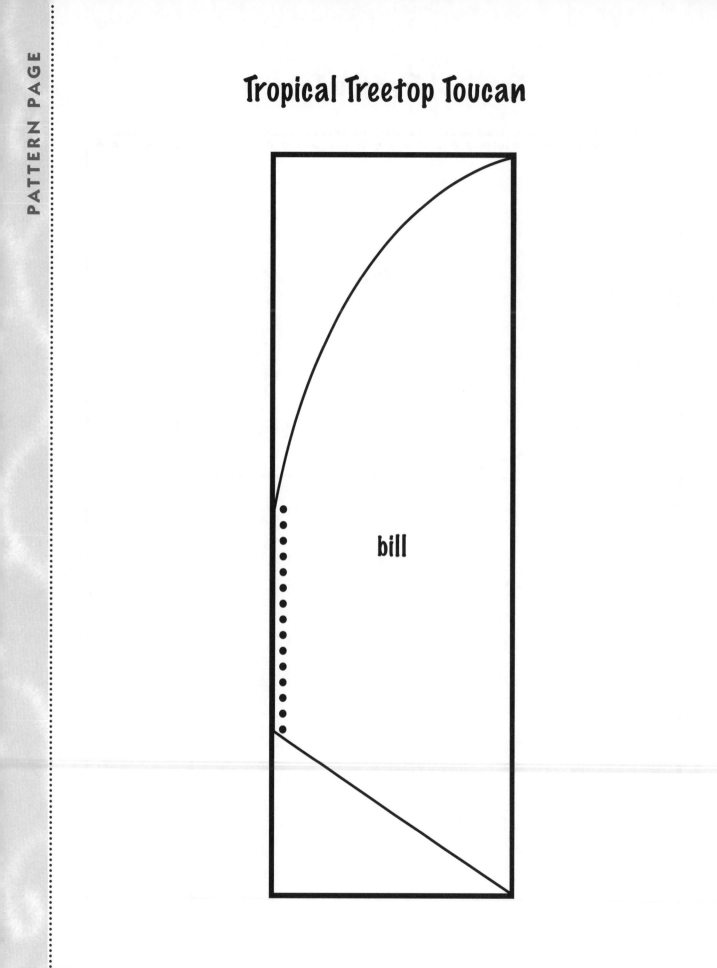

bill

Colorful Beetle

body

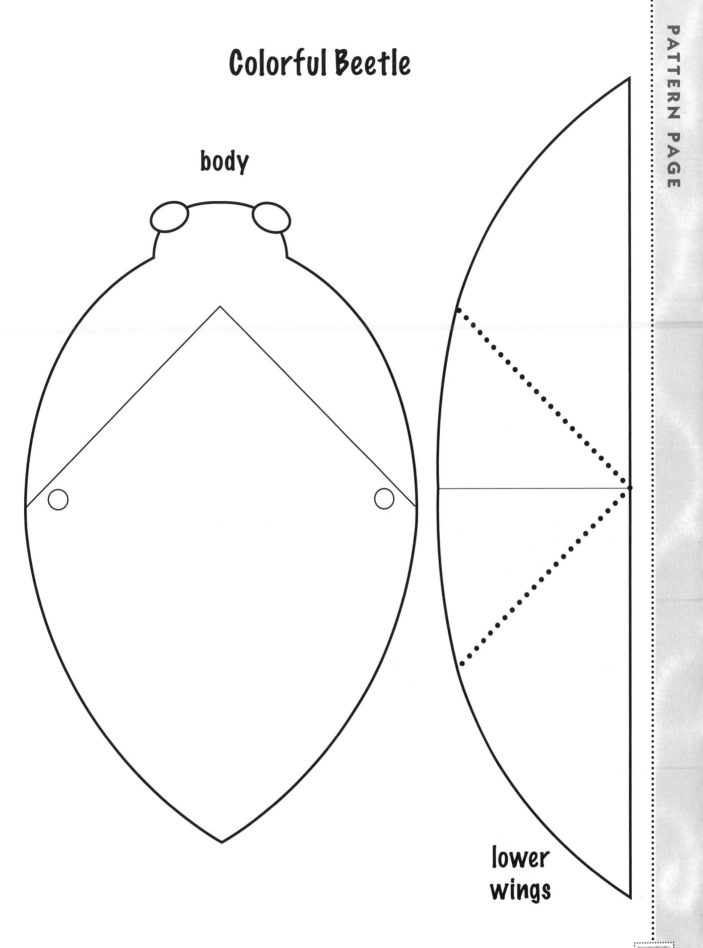

lower
wings

Amazing Animal Art Projects © 2008 by Jo Lynn Alcorn, Scholastic Teaching Resources

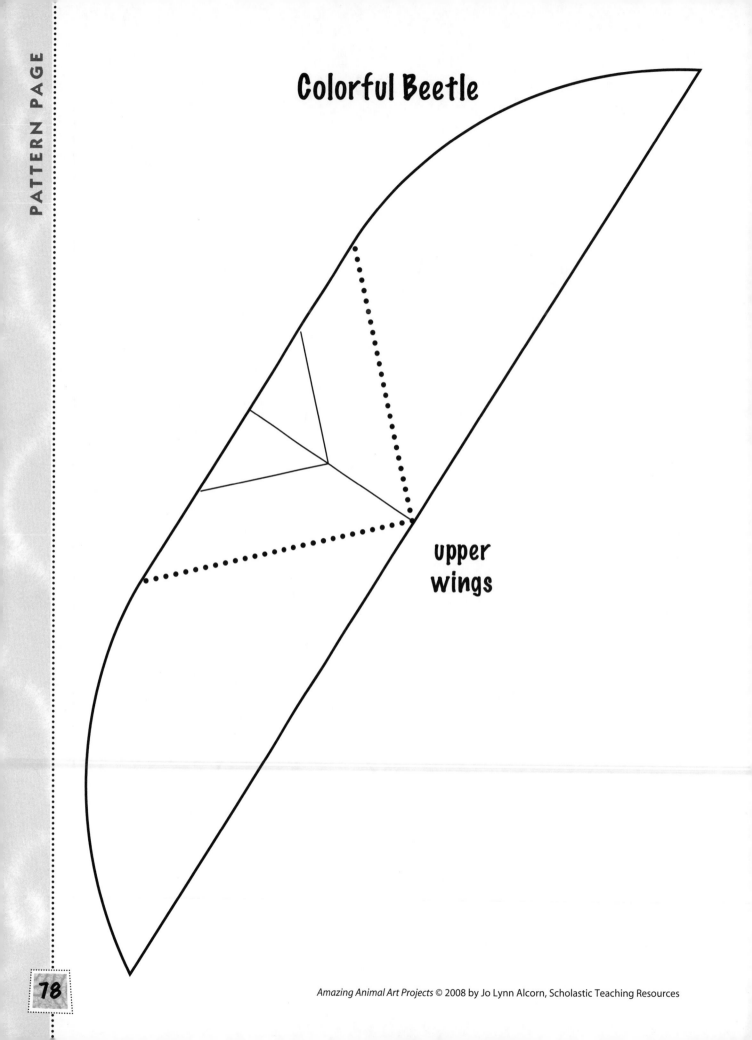

Colorful Beetle

upper
wings

Alligator Arm Puppet

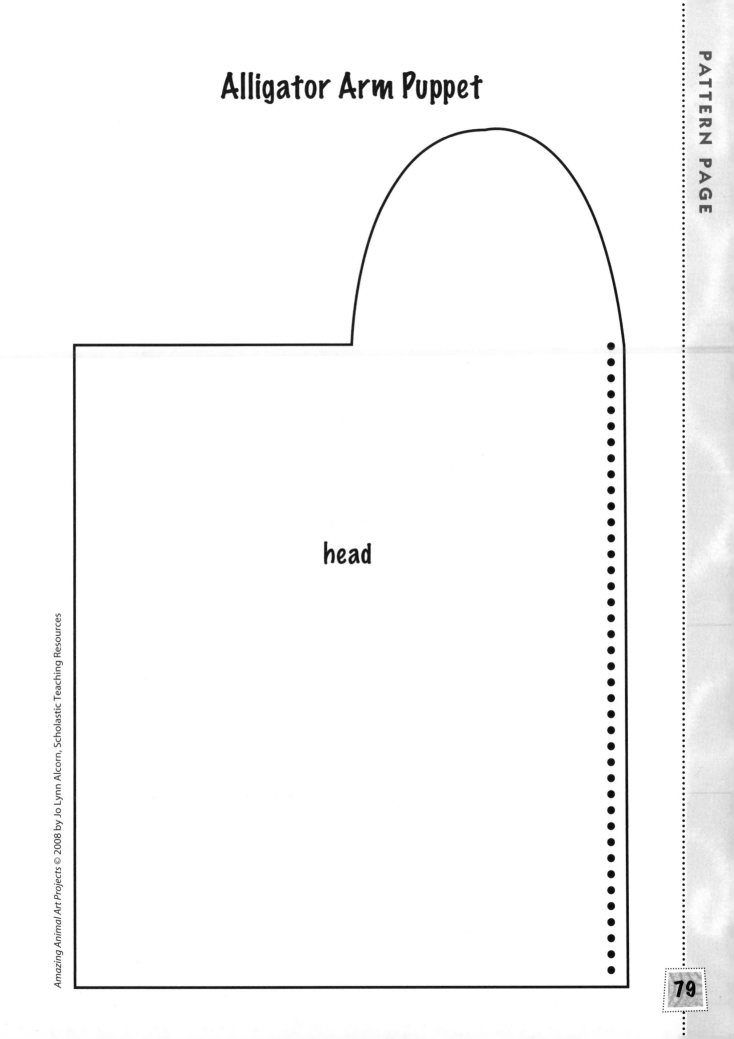

head

Slithery Snake

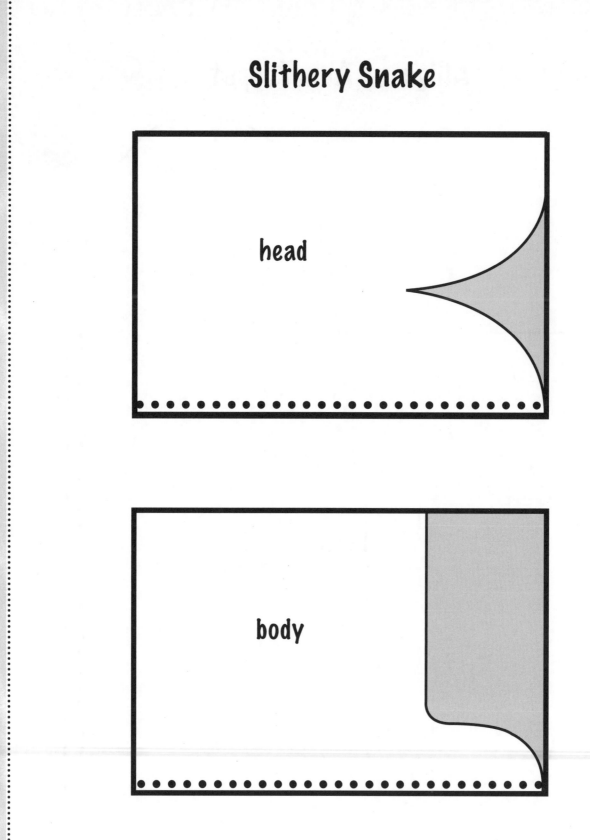

head

body